Sierra Stories

True Tales of Tahoe

Cover design and layout by *Riley Works*, Tahoe City, CA

Printed and bound in the United States of America

Library of Congress Catalog Number: 97-93297
ISBN: 0-9657202-1-7

Mic Mac
Publishing

P. O. Box 483 • Carnelian Bay, CA 96140
<www.MicMacMedia.com>

Sierra Stories

True Tales of Tahoe

by

Mark McLaughlin

Acknowledgments

No book is created in a vacuum. I thank the following people for all their help.

- William B. Berry, a good friend and inspiration, and at 94 years of age, the oldest working newspaperman in North America.

- Lee Mortensen and Phillip I. Earl, of the Nevada Historical Society.

- Guy Louis Rocha, Nevada Archives and Records Administrator.

- The friendly staff at the Getchell Library of the University of Nevada, Reno.

- Dohn Riley, of Riley Computer Services, for his critical eye, both in format and text.

About the Author

Mark McLaughlin, a professional researcher and writer with more than 300 published articles, trained as a historian and cultural geographer at the University of Nevada, Reno. McLaughlin's work appears regularly in California and Nevada newspapers; he was awarded the Nevada State Press writing award five times. Author of four books, McLaughlin frequently writes historical articles for such magazines *as Sierra Heritage*, *Nevada*, and *Weatherwise*. His work has also been published in the *Reno News & Review*, *Issues in Science & Technology*, and the Grolier Educational *2002 Science Annual*. McLaughlin is a professional lecturer, a frequent guest on regional television and radio programs, and has consulted for *The History Channel*.

BOOKS BY MARK McLAUGHLIN

Western Train Adventures: The Good, the Bad & the Ugly
Sierra Stories: True Tales of Tahoe — Volume 2
Turning the Corner: Energy Solutions for the 21ˢᵗ Century

For more information about Mark McLaughlin's books, audio tapes, and his extensive work as a weather historian for Nevada, California, and the Sierra Nevada, visit his website:
<www.MicMacMedia.com>

Dedication

Many thanks to my parents, Florence and John, for their support, both emotionally and materially.

Special thanks to John, Jim, Thomas and Kevin, for being the best brothers anyone could hope for.

" The history of a country is best told
in a record of the lives of its people."

— *Macaulay*

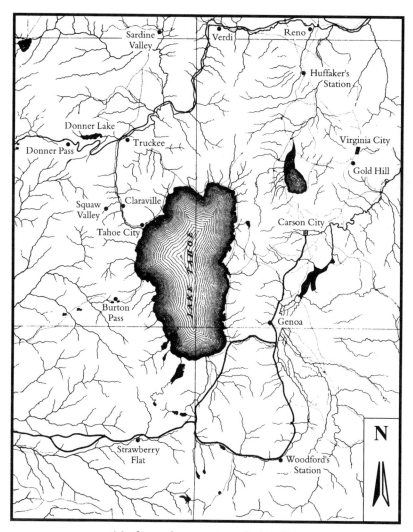

1 inch equals approximately 11 miles

Contents

Moses at Donner Lake

VISITORS TO DONNER LAKE hear all about the historic Donner Party tragedy that occurred there in the winter of 1846. Unfortunately, few learn the story of Moses Schallenberger, a teenage boy who survived a Sierra winter all alone at Donner Lake, two years before the Donner event.

Born in Ohio in 1826, Moses Schallenberger rode to California with the Stephens-Townsend-Murphy wagon train of 1844. Young Moses joined the Irish-dominated emigrant party with his older sister Elizabeth, and her new husband, Dr. John Townsend. The newly married couple had asked Moses to join them after his parents died of cholera. Dr. Townsend was taking Elizabeth west for her health and intended to become the first trained medical doctor in California.

There were fifty men, women and children in the Stephens Party when they organized at the frontier town of Council Bluffs, Missouri, in the spring of 1844. Half of them were members of the Murphy family, a large Irish clan, led by their patriarch, Martin Murphy, Sr. He was leading his family to California, where disease was rare and Catholicism was the country's official religion.

The emigrants elected as their captain Elisha Stephens, a forty-year-old blacksmith and former mountain trapper. Active, quick and untiring, Stephens was a born leader. He never wore a coat so all could see his sharp hunting knife, sheathed on his wide belt. He was tall, with piercing eyes, and exuded confidence and authority. His quiet, conservative temperament offset fears of rash or arrogant behavior. Stephen's leadership qualities were essential to the success of their journey.

In all, there were forty wagons rolling west that spring, but only the eleven wagons in the Stephens Party were heading for California. No one had ever taken wagons all the way west, over the Sierra and into the Sacramento Valley, but this small group of emigrants intended to try.

The group made good time traversing the vast, wind-swept prairie and then used the easy grade at South Pass, Wyoming, to cross the Rocky Mountains. Eighty-year-old Caleb Greenwood and his two half-Indian sons, John and Britton, had been hired as guides. Greenwood and his sons were experienced "pilots." The old man and his sons rode ahead on horseback and then reported back to the wagon train on the best route to follow. The skilled scouting by the Greenwoods enabled the heavily loaded wagons to roll west quickly.

Fear of Indian attack was high, especially when camps were made near wooded areas. Guards were posted over the cattle every night. Occasionally the boredom and monotony of guarding cattle against imaginary Indians inspired the young men in the group to play pranks. During one especially quiet night, John Murphy decided to play a joke on fellow pioneer John Sullivan. John attempted to enlist Moses Schallenberger in his conspiracy, but young Moses worried how the stern Martin Murphy Sr. might punish them for it. Just to be sure, they told Murphy Sr. their plan first; and he heartily endorsed it. While their victim slept, Murphy led some of Sullivan's cattle a short distance into the nearby woods and yelled, "Whoa! Indian attack!" Sullivan, who had been obsessed with the idea of a skirmish, jumped to his feet with his six-gun cocked and ready. John Murphy pointed out the missing cattle and off went Sullivan. After a long and exhausting chase, Sullivan captured his cattle and re-secured them to his wagon.

Sullivan had barely fallen back asleep when John Murphy shouted another warning. Sullivan couldn't believe it was his cattle stolen again. This time, Moses had driven the cows further than before and the only way they could be followed was by the subtle clinking of their yoke rings. To determine their whereabouts, Sullivan climbed to the top of a fallen log where he stood still, listening intently. John Murphy, who was hiding behind the log, saw Sullivan quietly standing there. Murphy held his loaded shotgun as close as he dared and fired into the sky.

Terror-stricken, Sullivan leaped into the air and ran at full speed back to the wagons, crying out that he had been shot by an Indian. In the meantime the cattle were quickly recovered and once again secured to the wagon. Moses and the Murphys' smiled quietly for weeks while Sullivan bragged about his "narrow escape" from hostile Indians.

In August, the Stephens Party said goodbye to their Oregon-bound friends and turned south off the well-traveled trail. Although saddened by the parting, it was with great determination that they rolled off into the trackless desert. The Bartleson-Bidwell Party had passed this way in 1841, as had the Chiles-Walker Party in 1843. But the earlier pioneers had abandoned their wagons before reaching California and their tracks were nowhere to be seen. The Stephens Party was on its own now. Even Old Caleb had never seen this desolate country before.

For six weeks they followed the westward-running Mary's River, later re-named the Humboldt, using its water and grass to sustain their oxen. Digger Indians, whose language was unknown to old Greenwood, inhabited the region. He managed to communicate with the Native Americans through signs and sketches drawn in the sand. Although the emigrants considered the Diggers "degraded and totally without energy," the Indians were very friendly, and every night hundreds of them visited the camp.

The Humboldt River is five hundred miles long, one of the longest rivers in the world that fails to reach an ocean. There is no lake at the end of the Humboldt, only a sink, or dry shallow depression in the arid landscape. A barren desert stretches to the horizon west of the Humboldt Sink. No wagons had ever crossed this waterless desert. The members of the Stephens Party were split on what to do. Should they abandon their wagons, carry what they can and walk south, as the Bartleson Party had done? Both Stephens and Greenwood knew that California was due west.

It was the first of October and the days were getting short. The first storms of winter were not far off. After a stressful delay of several days, they found an old Paiute Indian who told them to head west, straight across the forbidding desert. Chief Truckee used sign language and diagrams to show Greenwood that on the other side of the desert was a tree-lined river filled with fish. Fed by melting Sierra snow, this river flowed east out of the mountains.

John Murphy called the elderly Indian, "Truckee," because he replied to their questions with a word that sounded like "truk-ee." Truk-ee meant "everything will be alright." Chief Truckee told them to follow the river upstream; from there they could find their way west across the rugged Sierra and into California.

Despite Truckee's friendly attitude, Captain Stephens did not trust the old Chief. So, Stephens, Dr. Townsend, and a man named Joseph Foster, took the elderly Paiute with them to scout out the trail. But Chief Truckee was right and the cold, rushing river they found now bears his name. They crossed the Forty Mile Desert in two days and forced their oxen-drawn wagons up the steep Truckee River Canyon.

The precipitous cliffs of the canyon often forced them to march right in the river bed. The ancient river had eroded the banks so completely that one day they crossed it ten times in a mile. Constant immersion in the cold river water softened the oxen's hooves, causing them to split painfully. Nonetheless, the bawling cattle were forced ahead. To stop now meant terrible death in the winter snows. Increasing snow flurries attested to that.

In early November, they reached the lake now called Donner. Dark clouds cloaked the rugged mountain peaks and a foot of fresh snow already whitened the towering walls of granite. Winter was coming fast. Despite the intense urgency to cross the pass, Captain Stephens was forced to spend several days exploring the treacherous cliffs, searching for a way over.

While the main group waited for Stephens to find a suitable route, an advance party had decided to forge ahead and follow the Truckee River to its source. Six of them, young, strong and well-supplied, rode their horses south along the river. Mrs. Townsend joined this splinter group with her servant Francis Delanet in tow. Mr. Townsend stayed with the wagons. On November 16, this group reached the north shore of Lake Tahoe. They became the first white people to stand on the banks of this huge alpine lake. American Indians had hunted and fished at Tahoe for countless generations. (Kit Carson and John Fremont "discovered" the lake on Valentine's Day, 1844, just nine months before.)

The lead group on horseback had no time to enjoy the lake. They scrambled up the McKinney Creek canyon on Tahoe's west shore and then crossed the Pacific Divide. From there they descended down the Rubicon River canyon to the American River. They arrived safely at Sutter's Fort in the Sacramento Valley on December 10, 1844.

Meanwhile, back at Donner Lake, Stephens had found a small gap in the cliffs and given the order to move out. They decided to take five of the wagons and leave six at the lake. The wagons set to go were partially unloaded to lighten the load. While the men dismantled the wagons, the women and children carried the contents up to the summit. Snow had piled two feet deep and the footing was treacherous. Piece by piece, the wagons had to be pushed, pulled and dragged up the sheer granite walls. For each wagon the oxen had to be triple teamed. It was torture for man and beast.

Incredibly, by November 25, all five wagons had been hauled over the summit. They had become the first pioneer settlers to successfully take wagons over the Sierra and open the California Trail! They were over the divide, but still far from their destination. Vicious winter snowstorms plagued them as they struggled down the Sierran west slope. The oxen were too tired to pull the wagons through the deep snow and pregnant Mrs. Murphy had gone into labor. They set up a survival camp on the south fork of the Yuba River. It was there that Elizabeth Yuba Murphy was born.

Stephens realized that they could not survive a winter there. The men decided to make a break for Sutter's Fort to get help. They built a crude shelter and butchered some of the cattle for food. The women and children, as well as a couple of elderly men, were left in relative safety at the snowbound campsite. The rest of the men set out for Sutter's Fort, driving the remaining oxen ahead of them to break trail.

The men arrived at the fort seven days later. They found the horseback party already there, safe and sound. The men were anxious to return to the mountains to rescue their wives and children, but somehow John Sutter persuaded them to join his rag-tag army fighting in the "Micheltorena War." It wasn't until a month later that Stephens and some of the others could abandon the war effort and return to Sutter's Fort.

When the long-delayed rescue party finally returned to the camp on the Yuba River, the snowbound emigrants were near starvation. One family had eaten nothing but boiled rawhide for fourteen days. The fresh provisions gave the women and children the strength they needed to escape their snowbound camp. The food nourished them, but it still took the half-starved survivors twenty-one days to reach Sutter's Fort.

Meanwhile, Joseph Foster and Allen Montgomery had agreed to remain at Donner Lake and guard the wagons. Dr. Townsend and Moses Schallenberger had brought with them several trunks loaded with valuable goods, which they intended to sell for profit in California. Seventeen-year-old Moses volunteered to stay behind to protect their possessions. Although they were expecting only a short stay, the men wisely cut some saplings and built a crude cabin. They roofed it with animal hides and pine boughs. The three men planned to wait there until they were relieved by a rescue party.

All three men were fine marksmen in the best frontier tradition and wild game seemed plentiful. Confident in their hunting abilities, but ignorant of the deep drifts that bury the Sierra every winter, the mid-westerners never expected the snowdepth to exceed two feet. The first night they spent in their rough shack, it snowed three feet. The abundant game disappeared with the first snowflake.

Winter set in quickly and by the first day of December, the snow was nearly ten feet deep. The snow was so light and frosty, it would not bear their weight. Unfamiliar with basket-style snowshoes, the men could only flounder helplessly in the deep snow. Their food supply consisted of a few provisions and the two half-starved cows left behind. It wasn't long before the men realized that there would not be enough meat to last the winter.

In a fit of desperation, Foster and Montgomery constructed their own primitive version of the snowshoe. They bent half-inch-thick hickory wagon bows into an oblong shape forming a hoop. Across the hoop they wove a network of rawhide strips. Now they could walk on the snow, but there was nothing to hunt. Starvation stared them in the face.

After lengthy deliberation, they decided to make a dash over the snow-choked pass. For this desperate attempt, they each carried ten pounds of dried meat, a pair of blankets and a rifle with ammunition. They were in trouble from the start. The snowshoes were fastened to their boots so completely that accumulating snow could not spill off. With each step the weight grew greater. In a short time each shoe weighed about ten pounds.

Foster and Montgomery were mature men and could stand greater hardship than the adolescent Schallenberger. Moses tried to follow, but he was too weak from hunger and could not keep up. Severe leg cramps crippled Moses as he struggled through the drifts. The paroxysms of pain became more and more frequent until he could not walk more than fifty yards without stopping to rest.

They pushed through the snow for fifteen tortuous miles before darkness overcame them. That night they built a fire and collapsed from exhaustion. Moses was so stiff he could barely move. Sleep eluded the exhausted men as they contemplated their fate. During the night, their fire melted the snow in a circle fifteen feet wide and had sunk fifteen feet down to the ground. Moses saw the tremendous snowdepth as an ominous sign and he made his decision. He would return to the cabin.

Foster and Montgomery reluctantly agreed to their friend's plan. After a warm handshake and a sad goodbye, the two men headed west for Sutter's Fort. Moses started back down to Donner Lake. The snow had frozen overnight so Moses was able to walk without the cumbersome snowshoes, but his strength failed him as he approached the crude shelter. Despite a doorsill only nine inches high, he could not step over it without using his hands to raise his leg. He collapsed into bed, too tired to worry that his survival rested on his shoulders alone.

Moses was out hunting with first light. There were plenty of tracks, but no animals. He returned to the cabin discouraged and sick at heart. As he put his gun away in the corner, he noticed some steel traps that Captain Stephens had left behind. He baited the traps with some of his precious cow meat and placed them near the trails. The following day he inspected the traps and jumped for joy at his first catch, a half-starved coyote. His enthusiasm faded when he nearly choked on the bad-tasting meat and could not eat it. On the third night, however, he caught two foxes which he found delicious. Thereafter, his trapping was successful enough to hold off starvation.

Life in the dark, snowbound cabin was miserable for Moses. Wolves howling in the night interrupted his sleep and the daily struggle to survive wore him down. He constantly worried what he would do if he failed to catch a fox. He had enough coffee for just one cup. He saved it for Christmas. Fortunately, there were plenty of books to read from the small library that his brother-in-law, Dr. Townsend had left behind in his wagon.

Moses often read aloud in order to break the oppressive stillness.

On February 28, Moses Schallenberger saw something moving in the distance. It was his Canadian friend, Dennis Martin, who had come to rescue him. Martin had promised Elizabeth that he would save her younger brother if he was still alive. Martin fashioned new and improved snowshoes for the weak and emaciated Moses and helped him over the pass and down to the green, flower-studded Sacramento Valley.

Moses Schallenberger had spent three months alone in the snowbound Sierra and lived to tell the tale. By the time he was reunited with his family and friends it had been nearly one year since leaving Missouri. Despite all the hardships, there were no casualties in the Stephens Party. In fact, the well-led group was so successful that two babies were born during the journey, which increased their number to fifty two.

Today, Moses is honored by a mountain ridge just south of Donner Lake, known as Schallenberger Ridge.

CHAPTER ONE SELECTED SOURCES

Mary Lou Lyon, *Captain Elisha Stephens, 1804-1887, A True Pioneer*, Lyon Historical Enterprises, Cupertino, California, 1995.

Horace S. Foote, *Pen Pictures from the Garden of the World*, The Lewis Publishing Company, Chicago, 1888.

The Trinity Windows, a booklet from the San Jose Trinity Episcopal Church. Based on a work by Joan C. de Lisle., 1977.

Jim Rose, *Elisha Stephens*, article in Sierra Heritage Magazine, November/December, 1994.

Jim Rose, *Saga of the Stephens-Townsend-Murphy Party of 1844: First Pioneer Wagons Over the Sierra Nevada*, article in Nevada County Historical Society Bulletin, July, 1994.

Myron Angel, *History of Nevada*, Arno Press, New York, 1973.

Francis P. Farquhar, *History of the Sierra Nevada*, University of California Press, Berkeley, California, 1965.

Charles K. Graydon, *Trail of the First Wagons Over the Sierra Nevada*, The Patrice Press, St. Louis, Missouri, 1986.

George Stewart, *The California Trail, An Epic With Many Heroes*, University of Nebraska Press, Lincoln, Nebraska, 1962.

Hubert Howe Bancroft, *History of California Volume IV, 1840–45*, San Francisco History Company, 1886.

The Legendary Mailman
Snowshoe Thompson

"HE FLEW DOWN THE MOUNTAINSIDE. He did not ride astride his pole or drag it to one side as was the practice of other snowshoers, but held it horizontally before him after the manner of a tightrope walker. His appearance was graceful, swaying his balance pole to one side and the other in the manner that a soaring eagle dips its wings."

The words were penned by Dan De Quille, famed journalist for the *Virginia City Territorial Enterprise* and colleague of Mark Twain, but the inspiration came from a legendary Norwegian known as John "Snowshoe" Thompson. De Quille was not easily impressed, but after witnessing Snowshoe skiing down a steep mountain side with the grace of a ballet dancer, he was moved to eloquence. Early Sierran settlers had seen skis before, but nobody danced on the 25-pound oak boards like Thompson.

Thompson was only ten years old when he emigrated to the United States from Norway in 1837. John's family had sailed for America after his father died. Like many other Norwegians they settled in the Midwest and engaged in farming. In 1851, 24-year-old John was bitten hard by gold fever. He spent several years searching the Sierra for his El Dorado, but ultimately moved to Putah Creek in the Sacramento Valley of California, where he farmed in the summer and cut firewood in the winter.

During the long winter months, conversation often focused on the difficulty of getting mail in from the East. More than 100,000 men had invaded Northern California in the Gold Rush of 1849-51 and their most important link to the homeland was the letters which they sent and received. The demand for communication between West and East resulted in the establishment of mail routes between San Francisco and Salt Lake City in 1851.

The lucrative mail contract was worth $14,000 annually, but the brutal blizzards and deep snows of the Sierra Nevada made delivery by men and animals virtually impossible. Avalanches and weather delays forced the early carriers to ship the mail by steamer to Los Angeles and then eastward over the Old Spanish Trail through Arizona.

John Thompson imagined a better way. Web style snowshoes were rarely used in the Sierra, but a few early pioneers walked over the deep, loose snow on long, hand-carved wooden boards. Precursor to the modern snow ski, these crude contraptions were called snowshoes in the mid 1800's. Thompson remembered that as a young boy in Norway he and his friends had used long wooden skates to travel quickly over the snow-covered landscape. So Thompson carved himself a nice pair of oak skis. They were ten feet long, tapered in the middle, and four inches wide with curved-up tips.

It takes a strong man to control skis of such magnitude, but Thompson was the man for the job. He stood six feet tall and weighed a solid 180 pounds. With his blonde hair and beard, fair skin and blue eyes, he looked every bit the fierce Norseman of his ancestry. Thompson intended to ski the mail, as well as newspapers, medicine, and even ore samples back and forth, from Placerville, California to Genoa, Nevada. His pack weighed between 60 and 80 pounds. Later it would reach 100 pounds. His friends and neighbors feared that he would never make it. Ninety miles separate Placerville and Genoa, nearly all of it in the unforgiving winter conditions of the High Sierra.

But Thompson was determined. On his first trek eastward, he conquered the hazardous journey in just three days. The return trip back, up and over the Sierra's steep eastern escarpment, took him less than forty-eight hours!

Thompson never missed a delivery throughout the winters of 1856, 1857 and 1858. Fair skies or storm, rain or snow, Snowshoe Thompson always delivered. The fierce blizzards never delayed his departure although people often whispered that he would not be seen again until his frozen body was found in the spring. But, year after year, Snowshoe proved them wrong.

Thompson rarely made camp. He usually tucked himself into a small cave or lay on a bed of freshly cut pine branches. He built fires for heat, but when a blizzard made a fire impossible, he danced a jig on a flat rock to stay warm. Thompson often preferred to ski at night when the snow was hard, crusted and very fast. He navigated in the dark using the stars as a compass and he judged his progress and elevation by observing rock formations along the route.

Miners working the placer diggings of Gold Canyon on the east slope of the Sierra relied on Snowshoe Thompson to deliver their important letters and papers. Two Nevada miners, Peter O'Riley and Pat McLaughlin, told Thompson that they had run into heavy, blue rock flecked with gold. They had no idea what it could be.

In June, 1859, O'Riley and McLaughlin handed Snowshoe a sample of the ore. Thompson took it to Professor W. Frank Stewart, a geologist and mining expert, who was then editor for the Placerville *Weekly Observer.* Stewart was considered a great authority on minerals. Stewart immediately pronounced the blue stuff to be silver ore of the richest kind. He told Thompson to take the sample to Sacramento for another assay. In Sacramento the ore was declared to be black sulphuret of silver, and so rich that the assayer could hardly believe his figures. Word of the spectacular silver strike spread like wildfire, but Thompson, now a married family man, did not care. He had lost the stomach for mining.

During 1859, news of the Comstock discovery brought thousands of miners to Nevada, so Thompson expanded to operate horse-drawn passenger sleighs over the upper elevations of the Sierra. Over the years, Thompson continued to provide newspapers, mail, and essential medicines for the snowbound residents of the Eastern Sierra mining camps.

Thompson's skiing ability grew legendary, as did his confidence. At La Porte, in Plumas County, he challenged all other snowshoers to a race. He underestimated his competition when he took on the skilled Plumas County longboard racers. These men were experts at doping their skis. Famed snowshoer "Quicksilver" Hendel described dope as "the material used to lubricate the bottom of the shoes and cause them to glide over the snow. The object is to counteract friction as

SNOW SHOE RACES!

FOUR DAYS SNOW-SHOE RACING AT HOWLAND FLAT,

UNDER THE AUSPICES OF THE

TABLE ROCK SNOW-SHOE CLUB,

Commencing on Monday, March 15th, '69.

PROGRAMME.

First Day. 1st Race. Club Purse of $125 free for all. 2d Race. Entrance money of the day free for all but winner of the first race.
Second Day. Club Purse of $75, free for all. 2d Race. Entrance money, free for all but winner of the first race of this day.
Third Day. Club Purse $75, free for all. 2d Race. Entrance money, free for all but the winner of the first of this day.
Fourth Day. 1st race. Club Purse of $125 free for all. 2d race. Entrance money free for all but winner of first race this day.

Purses for Boys will be made up during the races. Racing to commence at precisely 1 o'clock. All entries must be made before 11 o'clock A. M. with the Secretary. Entrance fee $1. If the weather should prove unfavorable on Monday, March 15th, the Races will be postponed from day to day until favorable.

FREE DANCES DURING THE WEEK

and a GRAND BALL on St. Patricks Night

the 17th inst, at the SIERRA NEVADA HOTEL. During the week of the races the Sanhedrim of the Ancient and Honorable Order of E. C. V. located at Howland Flat, will, by permission granted by the G. R. N. H., have a celebration, procession etc.

By order of the Club.

Sam. Wheeler, Secretary.   **D. H. OSBORN, President.**

much as practicable." Dope recipes included varying amounts of sperm whale oil, oil of spruce, balsam fir, pitch pine, camphor and oil of tar. Thompson was unfamiliar with this crucial aspect of snowshoe racing and he paid the price for his ignorance.

Veteran racer Frank Steward defeated the renowned Norwegian and was proclaimed world champion by the miners. A quiet and chastened Snowshoe won the consolation title of greatest skier of them all, a tribute to his great survival skills and endurance. By winter's end, Thompson had learned his lesson. That April, the Alpine *Chronicle* reported, "On Sunday last, for the first time, Thompson used dope and made a run of 1,400 feet in 15 seconds: and on Monday last he climbed 300 feet higher and ran it in 22 seconds: he later ran 2,000 feet in 21 seconds." Apparently, Snowshoe enjoyed the exhilaration of racing as much as the challenge of the backcountry.

In the 19th century, western skiing styles and racecourse techniques were far different than today. Early skiers stood four abreast and raced at full speed, head-to-head, down a straight-away track nearly 2,000 feet long. Contestants often reached speeds in excess of seventy miles-per-hour. Falling over into the snow occasionally caused serious injuries to the racers, but the greatest risk lay in getting run over by another contestant.

The winning purse at a La Porte ski contest was $1,000, but the champion was expected to buy drinks for the crowd. The clamor for whiskey was so high at these races that one winner spent all his purse plus $2,000 besides, trying to quench the thirst of his fans. With so much money at stake, everyone wanted to compete. At St. Louis, Sierra County, a 9-year-old girl blasted through 300 feet of windswept powder in just seven seconds. A 14-year-old girl tucked straight down 1,230 feet in just 21 seconds, a speed equal to skiing one mile in a minute and a half!

The fastest time ever clocked at La Porte occurred in 1874, when Tommy Todd of the Alturas Snowshoe Club, rocketed down 1,804 feet in 14 seconds flat. Over the years, the races varied to include events comparable to the modern slalom, giant slalom, and cross-country. Thanks in part to Snowshoe

Thompson, La Porte can claim the distinction of being the birthplace of ski racing in the western United States.

For most of the years that Thompson carried the mail, he was paid little but promises. As he approached his 50th birthday, he petitioned the United States Congress for $6,000 in back pay. His petition was signed by all the state officials at Carson City. In order to plead his case in person, Thompson left Reno by train for Washington, D.C. on January 17, 1874. Three days later, the train stalled in a blizzard thirty-five miles west of Laramie, Wyoming. Undaunted by the severe winter storm, Thompson and a fellow passenger, Rufus Turner, of Idaho, hiked all the way to Laramie and boarded another eastbound train. After another day of storm delay, this train also failed to move, so the indomitable Snowshoe set out again. The storm had grown worse, temperatures ranged from fifteen to thirty degrees below zero. Turner realized he had had enough of the blizzard and decided to remain with the snowbound train.

Not a man to let a little snow bother him, Thompson turned up his coat collar and set out into the storm again. In two days he walked another 56 miles to Cheyenne, Wyoming, where he boarded a waiting eastbound train. This train beat the storm blockade and Snowshoe made it to Washington, D.C. He became the first man to arrive from the Pacific Coast in two weeks. Eastern newspapers declared Thompson to be the first man to beat the "iron horse" on such a long stretch. His sensational journey for payment proved fruitless, however, when Congress turned him down.

Thompson died in 1876 at age 49. It seems those years battling the Sierra Storm King had taken their toll after all. Three months before Snowshoe died, Dan De Quille interviewed the popular Norwegian. De Quille questioned

Thompson whether he had ever lost his way in the rugged mountains during all those years of storm and snow. Snow-shoe replied, "No, I was never lost — I can't be lost. I can go anywhere in the mountains, day or night, storm or shine." Tapping his forehead with his forefinger, he added, "I've got something in here that keeps me right. I have found many persons who were lost — dozens of men, but I have never been lost myself. There is no danger of getting lost in a narrow range of mountains like the Sierra, if a man has his wits about him!"

CHAPTER TWO SELECTED SOURCES

William Banks Berry, *The Lost Sierra*, Western SkiSport Museum, Soda Springs, California, 1991.

Richard A. Dwyer and Richard E. Lingenfelter, *Dan De Quille, The Washoe Giant*, University of Nevada Press, Reno and Las Vegas, Nevada, 1990.

Eliot Lord, *Comstock Mining and Miners*, Berkeley: Howell-North, 1959.

George Lyman, *The Saga of the Comstock Lode*, Charles Scribner's Sons, New York, 1934.

Virginia City *Territorial Enterprise*, June 6, 1875.

Hutchings' California Magazine, February, 1857, No. VIII.

William Banks Berry, *Snow-shoeing in the Sierra*, article in 1950 F.I.S. *Ski Program Manual*, World Ski Championships, National Ski Association of America.

Weekly Nevada State Journal, March 9, 1872.

Nevada Historical Review, Bicentennial Commission, David Basso, editor, 1976.

Sierra Bulletin, Snowshoe Thompson article, February, 1935.

Dan De Quille, *Overland Monthly*, October, 1886.

Nevada State Journal, December 17, 1869.

Alpine Chronicle, April, 1869.

Hon. Alphonzo Bell, *Congressional Record Proceedings and Debates of the 94th Congress, First Session*, Washington, July 10, 1975.

PHOTO CREDITS

Page 17   Portrait of John "Snowshoe" Thompson hangs in the Norwegian Embassy in Washington, D.C., William B. Berry Collection.

Page 19   Downieville *Mountain Messenger*, March 15, 1869.

Squaw Valley Squelches Secret to Silver Strike

THE CALIFORNIA GOLD RUSH had long since peaked by 1863, but countless western miners were still burning with gold fever. That spring a hot rumor flashed through the foothill mining camps. Word spread that veins of promising ore had been discovered at the mouth of Squaw Valley, high in the Sierra Nevada. A horde of 600 desperate miners invaded the valley, each one hoping to find his own El Dorado. Their dreams of instant wealth were shattered when an assay of the abundant red and yellow rock proved it to be worthless rhyolite. The sobering news squelched the gold rush along the Truckee River and sent the miners packing.

Few of them realized that this was not the first time that the mountains surrounding Squaw Valley had influenced mining history. Just six years before, the secret to the riches of the famous Comstock Lode was lost there, buried in the deep drifts of an early Sierran blizzard.

The story begins in 1849 when two brothers from Pennsylvania caught gold fever. Son of a Universalist clergyman, Ethan Allen Grosch was only twenty-three-years-old when he and his younger brother, Hosea Ballou, decided to join the California Gold Rush. Unwilling to make the long and tedious overland crossing, they sailed from Philadelphia on February 28, 1849, heading for Tampico, Mexico.

It took the ship almost a month to reach Tampico, a seaport in eastern Mexico. Along the way a severe storm struck their vessel and lightning shattered the mast. High winds drove the ship back on its course, but the excited brothers refused to let the danger dampen their enthusiasm. Worse was yet to come. Horses, mules and provisions were obtained in Tampico, but the journey overland through Mexico was still fraught with peril. Unbearable heat, a scarcity of water, bad roads, dysentery and malaria all took their toll on the gold-crazed Forty-Niners.

Despite their impatience to reach the gold diggings, the two brothers didn't reach San Francisco until the end of August. Hosea was seriously ill with malaria and dysentery, and much too weak to work. Ethan Allen took care of his younger brother until his health returned. They finally began prospecting in El Dorado County, California, during the summer of 1850.

In 1853, after several frustrating years in the gold diggings of El Dorado County, they crossed the Sierra Nevada, determined to find success at Gold Canyon, in the Utah Territory, now western Nevada. The Grosch brothers suspected that the dark ore in Gold Canyon was rich in silver, but the other miners figured it to be worthless lead and shoveled it aside. After three more years picking at the desert mountain slopes, the brothers found two potential ledges. In a letter dated November 3, 1856, they wrote home, "we found two veins of silver at the forks of Gold Canyon. One of these veins is a perfect monster." They staked a claim and named it "Pioneer."

There were about one hundred grizzled prospectors combing Gold Canyon in 1856. To a man they cursed the dark colored clay-like substance that stuck to their pans and clogged the riffles in their mining rockers. Unaware of the huge bonanza squishing beneath their boots they continued to hunt for their precious yellow nuggets. The slim pickings inspired little hope for the future, so these early miners spent most evenings betting their meager pouches of gold dust on card games or getting drunk on "tarantula juice."

Serious and secretive about their work, the quiet Grosch brothers kept to themselves. They rarely visited town, and then only to pick up a book or letter from home, delivered by Snowshoe Thompson, the legendary skiing mailman of the Sierra. Unlike most of the other miners, the Grosch boys were well-educated and had training in mineralogy and elementary chemistry. They built a small cabin on the outskirts of the little mining camp of Johntown, near the present town of Silver City. Crammed into their dark shack was a large collection of technical books on mining and geology, as well as two small furnaces, a bellows, some chemical-testing apparatus and various assayer's tools.

The studious brothers spent every night in their stone cabin, huddled over their books, beakers and ore specimens. The walls of the cabin glowed ruby red when the flames flared in the furnace. Clouds of bright sparks burst from the chimney every time they tested the ore. Assay methods were crude, the brothers derived silver samples by exploding the blue-black ore in damp gunpowder. Their research was a mystery to the other miners. Each day the brothers climbed higher up the slopes of Gold Hill, searching for samples of the heavy rock. While every other miner in the Washoe District kicked and cursed the mucky blue-stuff, the Grosch boys were discovering that Gold Hill was bursting with rich veins of silver-bearing quartz.

Privately, the brothers were beginning to speculate about the untold riches that would be theirs once they began to mine in earnest. In 1857, they wrote their father from Gold Canyon, "Our first assay was one-half ounce of rock; the result was $3,500 of silver to the ton, by hurried assay, which was altogether too much of a good thing. We assayed a small quantity of rock by crushing some from another vein. The result was $200 per ton. We have several other veins which are as yet untouched. We are very sanguine of ultimate success." The brothers each swore secrecy; no one else was told of their incredible discovery.

There was one problem, however. Once the surface or placer deposits are exhausted, the emphasis shifts to hard-rock mining, using picks, shovels and machinery. To develop their claim, the two brothers needed venture capital to buy the equipment and hire workers. No banker would loan them money unless they disclosed the nature of the investment. The Grosch brothers wanted all of Gold Hill for themselves. Each passing day put their secret at greater risk. Other miners were bound to find the Grosch's diggings eventually. The sneaky vagabond prospector, Henry Comstock, was already beginning to poke around their claims.

Every prospector knew the old Spanish proverb — "Para trabajar un amina de plata se necesita una mina de oro." Loosely translated it means, "It takes a gold mine to develop a silver mine." The Grosch brothers needed money desperately, but they would not give away their secret. They were obsessed with their dream of fantastic riches. In order to support themselves, Allen and Hosea returned to panning for the scarce and pitifully small gold nuggets. They had become penny-wise, but dollar-foolish.

Many of the miners spent winters at Mud Springs, El Dorado County, on the California side of the Sierra. At Mud Springs the Grosch brothers organized the Pioneer Silver Mining Company and hired Richard Bucke, a young Canadian, to work for them. Still, he was told nothing of the great veins of silver.

The brothers had one last hope for financial support. George Brown, a cattle-trader in Carson Valley, was a trusted friend. Ethan Allen wrote him of their fantastic $3,500 ore assay. Brown became an instant believer and replied that he would sell his business immediately and bring his life savings of $600. It might be enough to support them all until winter set in.

The Grosch brothers worked and waited, waited and worked. Weeks went by, but Brown failed to show up. In August, 1857, Hosea's rusty pick slipped and pierced his foot just below the ankle, making a deep and painful puncture. There was no physician at Gold Canyon so Hosea just washed the tender wound and then returned to work. But Hosea was undernourished and working too hard. Gangrene set in and the red line of blood poisoning soon traced its way up his lower leg. Hosea contracted "lock-jaw," a form of tetanus that contorts the face into a painful grimace. Thirteen days later, Hosea died with that fatal grin fixed on his face.

Then came more bad news. Thieves had attacked George Brown, found his $600, and murdered him for it. Ethan Allen was crushed, but he would not give up. He wrote his father, "I feel very lonely and miss Hosea very much—so much that at times I am strongly tempted to abandon everything and leave the country forever, cowardly as such a course would be. But I shall go on; it is my duty." Ethan Allen's family honor required that he return to Sacramento City, secure the necessary capital, and develop the mine his brother gave his life for.

Ethan Allen bundled up his assay reports and maps of the Gold Canyon veins in waterproof paper. He filled a sack with some promising ore samples and prepared for the long hike to

Sacramento. It was sunny and mild on November 20 when Ethan Allen Grosch and Richard M. Bucke said good-bye to Henry Comstock. Ethan Allen had asked the shifty old miner to watch the cabin and record-books in his absence. This request was akin to asking the fox to watch the chickens.

Grosch and Bucke slowly made their way west into the High Sierra. As they approached Lake Tahoe a severe snowstorm engulfed them. The snowflakes swirled around them so thickly that they soon lost sight of the Truckee trail in the deepening drifts. They made camp in Squaw Valley, but after several days their meager provisions were soon depleted. The two men decided that returning would be as difficult as proceeding west, so they forced their way up and over the mountains to California. Soon they were waist-deep in snow and stumbling blindly in a second storm. When Ethan Allen's precious bundle of maps began to get wet, he hid them in the hollow of a fallen pine tree. With his knife he cut a large X in the bark in order to find the log again.

They struggled on until they stumbled into a remote mining camp called the Last Chance. Both men's legs were frozen and gangrene was setting in. There was no doctor within miles and no ether for an anesthetic. The miners operated on Bucke with a saw and knife, but it was too late for Ethan Allen. In his delirium, Allen babbled about his brother Hosea, the blue stuff and his mining company. On the morning of December 19, 1857, Ethan Allen Grosch opened his eyes briefly and then died. The secret to the riches of Gold Canyon died with him.

The miners took up a collection for Richard Bucke and returned him to his family in Canada. He recovered his health and went on to study medicine in Europe before becoming one of the best nerve specialists in Canada. In later years Dr.

Bucke helped erect a small monument over the grave of his friend, but he never joined in a search for the fallen pine tree.

On January 28, 1858, just six weeks after Ethan Allen died in the snows of the Sierra, Henry Thomas Comstock and several others were out prospecting. The miners climbed above the drainage of Gold Canyon to a rock outcropping they named Gold Hill. It was there that Comstock and his cohorts discovered more placer deposits of gold. Excitement in the mining district picked up again. But the deceased Grosch brothers had held their secret tightly, and the other miners still had no idea that the mountain itself was riddled with thick veins of gold-and silver-bearing quartz.

The placer gold claims yielded between $15 to $20 daily, decent earnings in the 1850s, but Henry Comstock crowed that there were richer diggings ahead. Perhaps he knew that the Grosch brothers had been on to something big; he kept his eyes open. A tall, gaunt Canadian, Henry's nickname was "Old Pancake," a moniker his fellow miners bestowed on him. While most miners took the time to bake their flour into bread, "Old Pancake" believed he had no time for such luxuries. He preferred to quickly griddle pancakes instead, before heading out to prospect.

On June 8, 1859, two Irish miners hit the jackpot. For months, Peter O'Riley and Patrick McLaughlin had worked their way up the creek of a nearby canyon, making barely $2 per day. Discouraged, they decided to work the creekbed one more week before heading south to the new diggings on the Walker River. The following day, while digging out a water hole, they dug into a layer of "unusual-looking"coarse black sand. Ignorant of its composition and too tired to care, they dumped a few buckets worth of the matrix into their rocker. After they ran water over it, the bottom of the rocker was literally covered with gold. They dug further into the lode and began pulling out gold and silver by the pound. In one afternoon, they made $1,000!

That evening, they marked their claim with stones and stakes, and cleaned out their rocker. At that moment, Henry Comstock came riding up. Generally considered lazy and shiftless by the other miners, Comstock was still living in the Grosch's cabin and only managed to keep his claim going by hiring two Indians as laborers. "Old Pancake" saw the glint of gold and threw himself to his knees to inspect the ore more closely. Suddenly, he stood up and coolly informed the astonished men that they were trespassing on his land. Henry Comstock had no title to the land or, more importantly, legal claim to the water, but he managed to convince O'Riley and McLaughlin that he did. Through bluster and bravado, Henry etched his name onto the richest silver strike in American history, the Comstock Lode.

Fame is fleeting, as an 1875 Storey County Mining Directory attests, "If the lode had been called after the first discoverer it should have been named the 'Grosch lode,' for the brothers located claims for themselves and others thereon long before the days of Virginia and Gold Hill were known."

CHAPTER THREE SELECTED SOURCES

Eliot Lord, *Comstock Mining and Miners*, Berkeley: Howell-North, 1959.

Richard A. Dwyer and Richard E. Lingenfelter, *Dan De Quille, The Washoe Giant*, University of Nevada Press, Reno and Las Vegas, Nevada, 1990.

Ray Allen Billington, *The Far Western Frontier 1830–1860*, University of New Mexico Press, Albuquerque, New Mexico, 1956.

Dan De Quille, (William Wright), *The Big Bonanza*, Alfred A. Knopf, New York, 1947.

Myron Angel, *History of Nevada*, Oakland, California, 1881.

William H. Brewer, *Up and Down California in 1860-1864*, Edited by Francis P. Farquhar. Berkeley: University of California Press, 1974.

Edward B. Scott, *The Saga of Lake Tahoe*, Crystal Bay, Lake Tahoe, Nevada, Sierra-Tahoe Publishing Co., 1980 printing.

George D. Lyman, *The Saga of the Comstock Lode*, Charles Scribner's Sons, New York, 1934.

Helen S. Carlson, *A Geographical Dictionary*, University of Nevada Press, Reno, Nevada, 1974.

Warren Hinckle and Fredric Hobbs, *The Richest Place on Earth*, Houghton Mifflin Company, Boston, Massachusetts, 1978.

Virginia City *Territorial Enterprise*, June 6, 1875.

Gold Hill *Evening News*, June 28, 1865.

Heroes of the Pony Express

IN THE EARLY WEST there had always been a strong desire to bring the mail overland, from Salt Lake City, Utah Territory, to Sacramento, California. The trail was 750 miles long, desolate and dangerous to the extreme. Pioneer travelers on the route encountered steep, rugged mountains and waterless deserts, scorching heat and deadly blizzards. It was also American Indian country, which added its own element of danger. For most, it was a journey endured only once.

The route started southeast from Salt Lake City, detoured around the Great Salt Lake, and then turned west across the Great Basin. The trail followed the meandering Humboldt River until it crossed the Forty Mile Desert into Carson City. California-bound travelers then climbed over the Sierra Nevada via the old emigrant road, and passed through Placerville, before arriving at Sacramento.

The most dangerous sections of the route were in Nevada and the Sierra. During winter, the Sierran portion of the trail was often buried in snow fifteen to twenty feet deep. In the spring, the usually humble Carson and Humboldt Rivers flooded from snowmelt. The only way across the rampaging rivers was by swimming; there were no bridges. Farther out in the desert, Shoshone Indians often attacked the mule trains, killing the men and plundering the mail.

Despite the known risks on the route, the United States government managed to negotiate a contract for mail delivery in 1851. The government wanted the mail delivered each way, once a month. First to tackle the formidable task were Colonel Absalom Woodward, and his partner, Major George Chorpenning, Jr. The name of their company was A. Woodward & Co., but most Westerners jokingly referred to it as the "Jackass Line." The unsavory moniker was born from the fact that mule trains were used to transport the mail. Mules are stubborn, but possess great endurance. For several months the Jackass Line was successful with the long-distance deliveries. The two men knew if they failed to deliver on schedule, no matter what the excuse, they would lose their lucrative government contract.

Luck ran out in November, 1851, when Woodward's train was attacked by hostile Indians along the Humboldt River. All of Woodward's men were killed and the mail was torn and scattered. Mortally wounded, Woodward managed to escape on a fast horse, heading east through Hasting's Cut-off. Woodward pushed on for 300 agonizing miles, but died from exposure and loss of blood, just 35 miles from Salt Lake City. His body was not found until spring.

Fortunately for Chorpenning, human memory is short-lived. The following year he managed to hire five new men to haul the mail east to Salt Lake City. Deep snow that spring forced the men to use Beckwourth Pass via the Feather River Canyon. The men and their pack animals were caught in a series of late-season blizzards near the pass and every mule in the train was frozen to death. The men pushed on in a forced march for 200 miles, surviving on mule meat for fifty-three days. Dedicated and determined to live, the five men carried the mail on their backs, all the way to Salt Lake City.

After that near-fatal incident, no one in Salt Lake City was willing to carry the mail, so Chorpenning was forced to lead the mule train to Sacramento alone. He hid during the daytime and traveled at night to avoid attacks by hostile Indians. Miraculously, he made it to California alive. By the end of 1852, the Central Route's reputation for hardship and death had become so notorious, that no one in California would work the Chorpenning line. The Federal government finally allowed the hapless Major to shift the route south, from Los Angeles east into southern Nevada and then northeast into Utah.

Several other methods of transporting the winter mail through the Great Basin were tried over the next few years. In the fastness of the snowbound Sierra, cross-country skiers were used, as were horse-drawn sleighs, dog teams, even horses wearing snowshoes. But the strangest experiment of all occurred in 1855, when Secretary of War Jefferson Davis, insisted on the use of camels in the desert. Davis managed to convince Congress that the dromedary, so accustomed to traveling for days without water, was perfect for the arid Nevada landscape. Jefferson also felt that the camels could be useful for military and mining purposes.

Congress funded a small naval expedition which was quickly dispatched to the Arab nations along the Mediterranean. After eight months, this naval "Noah's Ark" returned with nearly one hundred camels. Unfortunately, unforeseen problems kept cropping up with these beasts of burden. Horses and mules always stampeded at the sight and smell of the large alien creatures. The feisty camels attacked pedestrians with nasty bites and chewed the laundry off residents' washlines. In Virginia City, the strange camel trains were only allowed to pass through town at night. Nevadans hated the troublesome beasts. In Lyon County, if you let your camel stray, they threw you in jail for thirty days.

As it turned out, the camel project was a failure. The sharp rocks of the Great Basin cut their feet and despite special leather boots made to protect them, the stubborn camels refused to cooperate further.

As the Civil War approached, official interest in the Camel Corps waned and many were auctioned off. Some of the camels were recruited into circus acts; others were used by private freight-hauling and road construction outfits. Eventually, many of the poor beasts were abandoned in the desert, where some survived for years. Angry Wells Fargo drivers complained of camels all the way from Tahoe to Ely. Their teams panicked at every encounter with the strange, humped creatures. Even thirty years later, some wide-eyed prospector would stride into a Comstock saloon, belly up to the bar and tell the bartender of the bizarre "mirage" he had seen.

In 1859, after the camel corps fiasco, California Senator William H. Gwin and businessman William Hepburn Russell toyed with the idea of a relay system using young men on fast horses. Senator Gwin promised to garner Congressional support if Russell, known as "the Napoleon of the Plains" because of his grandiose business schemes, would offer his organizational skills. They called their novel delivery system the Pony Express. Advertisements were placed in newspapers — "YOUNG, SKINNY, WIRY FELLOWS, not over eighteen. Must be expert riders willing to risk death daily. Orphans preferred. WAGES $25 per week." Despite the obvious risk involved, nearly two hundred young men applied for the job. Only eighty made the cut.

Regardless of the weather, Pony Express riders were expected to make the run from Sacramento to Salt Lake City in three and a half days, and on to St. Louis within ten days. There were relay stations every twenty-five miles and each rider cov-

ered seventy-five miles in a run. Riders were expected to average at least ten miles-per-hour, regardless of terrain. They were allowed only two minutes rest at each station.

This elaborate enterprise included 500 sleek horses, but before an anxious rider could slip into the small racing saddle, he was stripped to the last ounce. At least the young man was permitted to carry a knife and a revolver in order to protect himself. Speed was of utmost importance, the mail bags never weighed more than twenty pounds. Every letter was written on thin tissue paper and the minimal postage was a costly five dollars. Once in operation, the Pony Express became the last link in a non-stop line of communication to span the continent.

Of all the Pony Express routes, none was more treacherous than the run between Sacramento and Carson City. Weather in the Sierra Nevada can be the worst in the country. Nearly forty feet of snow falls there in an average winter, sometimes more. The mail was first shipped by steamer from San Francisco, up the Delta to Sacramento, where an eastbound messenger picked it up. After that, the boys and their ponies took over.

The maiden run of the Pony Express began with a big celebration on the afternoon of April 4, 1860. All of San Francisco turned out to cheer the steamer *Antelope* when it departed the city by the bay and steamed out into the Sacramento River Delta. Ten hours later, at 2:45 in the morning, William (Sam) Hamilton, was waiting impatiently on a rain-soaked Sacramento dock. The *Antelope* was more than two hours late and Sam was worried about his buddy, Warren Upson. Warren had the run following his.

It had been raining for days in Sacramento and a blizzard was raging in the mountains. It would be nearly impossible for Warren to carry the mail through the blinding snowstorm at all, let alone on time. As soon as the little side-wheeler steamer bumped the pier, Sam grabbed the mail pouch and was on his way. Despite the rain, darkness and muddy road, he pushed his white mustang to full speed. His route followed what is now Highway 50, past Folsom, Placerville and on to Sportsman Hall. Sam Hamilton drove his horses hard. He tore through the 20 miles of mud and darkness in just 59 minutes — a fast ride on a dry road in daylight.

The rain fell in sheets as Sam's horse climbed the west slope of the Sierra. It was impossible to see, so Sam let his pony follow the trail by instinct. Each of his three mounts went down, but neither Sam nor the ponies were injured. Sam raced up Hangtown Gulch, a climb of 2,000 feet, and arrived at Sportsman's Hall at dawn.

Hamilton's relief, Warren Upson, whose father was editor of the *Sacramento Union*, grabbed the mail pouches from his exhausted friend. Through stinging sleet mixed with snow, Upson forced his horse through the rain-swollen American River and then up the west flank of the Sierra. Upson heard his pony snort in discouragement when the rain and sleet changed to snow. He pushed his horse through Hope Valley and then into Strawberry Valley. The powerful animal fought snow depths to its chest, but at times, Upson had to dismount and pull his floundering horse through the drifts.

Hour after hour the man and his steed fought the blizzard. At last, both stumbled into Friday's Station, the end of their route. Warren Upson had carried the first eastbound mail 55 miles over the snow-choked Sierra Nevada in just eight hours. That batch of mail arrived in St. Louis, Missouri, nine days later and right on time.

Several Pony Express riders became famous for incredible feats of endurance. In western Wyoming, "Wild Bill" Cody rode 320 miles in 21 hours and 40 minutes. The purported record was along the Nevada route when Robert (Pony Bob) Haslem rode 380 miles non-stop. Although these fearless young men pushed themselves to the limit, the entire 2,000-mile trip still took ten days in summer and fifteen days in winter. The fastest trip ever, occurred when riders carried President Lincoln's inaugural address west, in March of 1861. The entire run was accomplished in just seven days and 17 hours!

Despite its legendary fame, the Pony Express was a short-lived phenomenon. The transcontinental telegraph, hailed as the new electric highway, was completed on October 24, 1861. The electric telegraph signaled the end for the Pony Express.

From the Pony's first run on April 3, 1860, until its last on November 20, 1861 — a span of barely nineteen months — the riders covered some 616,000 miles, enough to circle the earth twenty-four times. The Pony Express existed for only a brief period of time, but the brave boys and their ponies will never be forgotten.

CHAPTER FOUR SELECTED SOURCES

Hubert Howe Bancroft, *History of Nevada, 1540-1888*, University of Nevada Press, 1981, Reno, Nevada.

George Lyman, *The Saga of the Comstock Lode*, Charles Scribner's Sons, New York-London, 1934.

Arthur King Peters, *Seven Trails West*, Abbeville Press, New York, 1996.

Myron Angel, *History of Nevada*, Arno Press, New York, 1973.

Lucius Beebe and Charles Clegg, *U.S. West; The Saga of Wells Fargo*, Bonanza Books, New York, 1949.

The Genoa-Carson Valley Book, Bicentennial Issue, 1976.

San Francisco *Daily Alta California,* May 8, 1860.

Sparks Tribune, January 3, 1952.

The Sacramento Bee, February 4, 1960.

Harper's Weekly, June 30, 1877.

PHOTO CREDITS

Page 39   *Harper's Weekly*, June 30, 1877, engraving by Paul Frenzeny.

Page 43   *Harper's Weekly*, November 2, 1867, engraving from a painting by George Ottinger.

Squaw Valley Gold Rush 5

Go for the Gold! During the 1960 Winter Olympics, athletes from around the world descended on Squaw Valley with the hope of taking home a gold medal. Many did.

During the summers of 1862 and 1863, between 2,000 and 3,000 men rushed to Squaw Valley, also with high hopes of getting their gold. But these men were not going to ski, skate or jump for it, they were going to mine it. Or so they thought.

In 1862, two prospectors, John Keiser and Shannon Knox, decided to leave the exhausted gold diggings in California, and head east for the Comstock mines in western Nevada. They coaxed their heavily-laden burros through the Sierran high country and then made the descent into Squaw Valley. The two men were an unlikely pair. Keiser was a miner from Germany, while Knox was a carpenter by trade from Pennsylvania. When the two men reached a flat near the Truckee River, just northwest of the mouth of Squaw Creek, they noticed some outcroppings of a rich-looking reddish ore. When they explored further up the river, more of the promising color was found.

Squaw Valley had never been known for gold. Generations of Washoe Indians had camped there in the summer and considered the valley sacred. After a long, cold winter in the Nevada desert, the bountiful deer, fish and grasses revived the emaciated tribe.

In 1862, the area was designated Federal land and open for settlement. Four enterprising men, Fish, Ferguson, Smith and Coggins, set up a small ranching operation on the valley meadows. They named their spread Squaw Valley Ranch. The name Squaw Valley originally came from a group of early Gold Rush emigrants who traversed the valley in the summer of 1849. As they passed through, they discovered many Americans Indians camped in the lush valley, but saw that all the male warriors were away hunting for deer. These emigrants noticed that there were only women and children left at the summer encampment, hence the name Squaw Valley.

The news of the Squaw Valley gold strike started a stampede of hopeful miners from the various encampments on the Sierra's west slope. Hard-working silver miners in the booming Washoe District paid little notice to this new find, but the rush threatened to depopulate much of Placer County. Merchants, miners, saloon owners and gamblers scrambled up and over the mountains and made a beeline for the new El Dorado. Rumors had it that this rich ore would even surpass the famous Comstock Lode itself.

Many of the placer deposits in the California foothills had played out by the early 1860s and hope for another new strike was on everyone's mind. In addition to the personal craving for wealth, the Civil War was in full swing and any new silver and gold deposits would be helpful to pro-Union interests. Most western miners were Union sympathizers.

More rumors spread that the gold-bearing quartz veins running through the valley were of an extraordinary thickness, with some of them touted as two hundred feet wide. Two of the richer ledges were named the "Vicksburg" and the "General Meade." An early assay of the ore from the "Vicksburg" mine reported $440 worth of gold per ton with strong potential for great profit.

By 1863, there were at least one thousand claims staked out and some thirty or forty mines were already incorporated.

Sec 6   Sec 5   Sec 4   Sec 3   Sec 2

A 620.04   A.643.24   A 637.92   A 637.18   A 640.32

160   160   160   160   160   160   160

4.000   79.75   80.42   79.81   80.32

West   N89°32'E   N89°52'E   N89°47'E   N89°42'E
160   Brook

Sec 7   Sec 8   Sec 9   Sec 10   Sec 11

A 624.28   640   640   640   640

160   Yellow Pine Sec Cor   Meadow

4.000   79.80   80.31   80.20   79.91

West   N89°34'E   S89°47'E   N89°40'E   N89°46'E
160

Sec 18   Sec 17   Brook   Sec 16   Sec 15   Sec 14

A 632.20   640   Firtree 640   640   640

160   Red Fir   Pitch Pine

79.52   79.63   80.00   Rocky Point   80.61   79.83

S89°28'E   N89°38'E   N89°54'E   S89°54'E   N89°51'E
160   Red Fir   Brook   Truckee River   Red Fir

Sec 19   Sec 20   Sec 21   Sec 22   Sec 23

A 640.00   640   640   640   640

160   Firtree   Pitch Pine   Knoxville Deserted Mining Town   Red Fir

20.79.50   79.73   80.37   79.63

N89°39'E   S89°43'E   S89°41'E   S89°54'E
160   High Quartz Ledge

Sec 30   Sec 29   Sec 28   Sec 27   Sec 26

A 320.00   640   640   640   640

160   Pitch Pine   Squaw Valley   Claraville Deserted Mining Town

4.000   79.32   79.80   80.46   79.50

West   N89°34'E   N89°51'E   S89°46'E   N89°47'E
160

Sec 31   Sec 32   Sec 33   Sec 34   Sec 35

A 160.00   640   640   Bear Creek   640   640

80   80   80   80   80

High Ridge   Brook   Brook   N17°27'E

Granite Mountains   High Ridge

Surveys Designated	By Whom Surveyed	Date of Contract	Amount of Surveys	When Surveyed
Township lines	E. Dyer	May 24th 1865.		1865
Offset to Township lines (brown)	" "	" "		1865
Rest of Section lines	" "	" "	55 m/s 39 chs. 81 ks.	August 26th 1865

Four mining districts were organized — Summit; Red, White & Blue; Border Line; and Soda Springs. Three small towns were laid out in the valley and along the Truckee River. The first town was called Knoxville, built near the mouth of Squaw Creek, named for Shannon Knox, one of the first prospectors. Tahoe City sprouted up near the outlet of Lake Bigler, later called Lake Tahoe. Claraville blossomed between the two of them, right on the Truckee River. A fourth mining camp, Elizabeth City, sprung-up five miles east, in the Martis Valley. Speculation in mining footage sent the price of town lots soaring, from $10 apiece to $200.

The new encampments transformed a primitive wilderness into a thriving commercial venture virtually overnight, but the miners were in no way enjoying luxurious accommodations. Like most early mining camps, these fledgling settlements were comprised of crude shacks with no windows, where hotels had dirt floors and no beds. After seeing the Union Hotel in Knoxville, one man declared that, "You could see clean through the walls and its roof was equally divided between canvas and bushes." Furniture had to be crafted on the spot and Main Street was too narrow for even a horse and wagon.

According to William H. Brewer's book, *Up and Down California in 1860 – 1864*, not everyone was caught up in the gold fever. One shrewd observer claimed: "I surely would not invest in any mine I have seen there, and I have visited eight or nine of the best. I'd give $25 for a good photograph of both main streets, particularly if it included Knoxville's Union Clothing Store, a shanty in the shade of a tree with brush for a roof." Nearly 600 anxious miners were working the diggings, but not one woman or child was to be found.

Like most mining towns in the 19th century, the pioneers enforced the law their own way, usually with a gun. When Tennessee outlaw, Johnson King, terrorized Knoxville and refused to pay for his purchases at the local store, shopkeeper James Tracey calmly pulled out his pistol and shot King between the eyes. Storekeeper Tracey may have lost a customer, but he did live to tell the story.

Late that fall, word came back on the ore specimens sent to Sacramento. It was a miner's worst nightmare. The assay report stated that the yellow ore was worthless, there was no gold at all! The strike was a bust. Some miners believed that Shannon Knox had salted his claim, but Knox had been digging as earnestly as anyone else.

The bonanza was over and, within a few days, the towns were deserted. All except for Tahoe City that is. Tahoe City eventually became the gateway to the whole Lake Tahoe Basin, first by stage, then by narrow gauge railroad. Several frustrated miners gave up the search for gold and settled along the west shore of Lake Tahoe. Each lent their name to the geography of the region — Ward Creek is named for Ward Rush, Blackwood Creek for Hampton Craig Blackwood, McKinney Creek for John McKinney and Burton Creek for Homer D. Burton.

CHAPTER FIVE SELECTED SOURCES

William H. Brewer, *Up and Down California in 1860-1864*, edited by Francis P. Farquhar, Berkeley, University of California Press, 1974.

Eliot Lord, *Comstock Mining and Miners*, Berkeley; Howell - North, 1959.

Edward B. Scott, *The Saga of Lake Tahoe*, 9th edition, Sierra-Tahoe Publishing Co., 1980.

Gold Hill *Daily News*, November 2, 1863.

The Strange Tale of Charley Parkhurst

IN THE EARLY DAYS AT LAKE TAHOE, heavy November snowstorms signaled the end of the busy stagecoach season. The deepening drifts usually forced most horse-drawn carriages to travel alternate routes during the winter months. Sometimes the narrow wheels were replaced with well-polished wooden runners, so that trained horses wearing snowshoes could pull the stage as a sleigh. Despite the stage-to-sleigh innovation, blinding Sierra snowstorms often made the journey impossible anyway.

Stagecoach companies were big business during the silver boom years and one of the most successful was the Pioneer Stage Company. The Pioneer Stage Line followed the old trail between Placerville, California, and Genoa, Nevada. The company maintained twelve superb Concord Coaches with six horses to each stage. Business was brisk. On average, more than 100 passengers used the line daily to reach Virginia City from California. Besides passengers, the stages hauled gold and silver bullion as well as mine company payrolls.

Stage robbery was a constant danger in the days before law and order arrived in the west. Bandits employed many strategies to ambush a stagecoach. The most common method was for the highway robbers to hide behind a thicket of trees or lay flat on the ground. When the stage approached, the crooks would jump to their feet with their guns drawn. Thieves rarely met with much resistance from the stage drivers, since the drivers had passenger safety foremost in mind. The gang was usually after the Wells Fargo box with its valuable contents.

Passengers were seldom hurt, but they were certainly relieved of their cash, watches and jewelry. If the bandits had time, the boot would be ripped open and the baggage and trunks searched.

"Gentleman Jack" Davis was the slickest of all the local highway- robbers. During one hold up, Davis spread Buffalo robes on the ground and served champagne and hors d'oeuvres to the passengers while his men blew up the money box. Bandits were often as nervous as the passengers. One saloon owner saved his watch and money by passing his whiskey bottle around among the thieves.

Before the completion of the transcontinental railroad over Donner Pass in 1868, the only transportation over the Sierra was by horse-drawn stagecoach. Throughout the spring, summer and fall, rugged teamsters held rein over six wild-eyed horses as they tore along the precipitous mountain trails. The beautiful alpine scenery passed by in a dizzying blur. Curious passengers who looked out of the open carriage windows often turned pale with white-knuckled fear. Sheer granite cliffs towered over the crude narrow trails and abyssal canyons yawned far below.

An article in the Omaha *Herald* in 1877 suggested some travel tips for stagecoach passengers;

"The best seat inside a stage is the one next to the driver. Even if you have a tendency to sea-sickness when riding backwards...you will get over it and will get less jolts and jostling. When the driver asks you to get off and walk do so without grumbling, he won't request it unless absolutely necessary. If the team runs away...sit still and take your chances. If you jump, nine out of ten times you will get hurt. Never shoot on the road, as the noise might frighten the horses. Do not discuss

politics or religion…and do not imagine for a moment that you are going on a picnic."

In fairness to the drivers, or whips as they were called, stage-coaches were kept on a strict time schedule and speed was of the essence. Passenger comfort was not a priority. It was considered a disgrace if a driver brought his stage in 30 minutes late. Despite wind, rain and snow, the mail and passengers were always rushed to their destinations. The stagecoaches were driven by skilled and fearless men who pushed themselves and their spirited horses to the ultimate limit.

One of the most famous drivers was Charles Darkey Parkhurst. Charley came west from New Hampshire in 1852, seeking his own fortune in the Gold Rush. He spent the next 15 years running stages in both California and Nevada. Over the years, his reputation as an expert whip grew legendary. Charley handled all six reins plus the whip with an easy dexterity. From 20 feet away, he could slice open the end of an envelope or cut a cigar out of a man's mouth. Parkhurst smoked cigars, chewed wads of tobacco and exuded supreme confidence behind the reins. His judgement as to what could and could not be done with a coach was always sound, and his pleasant manners won him friends everywhere.

One time, as Charley braked his stagecoach down a steep mountain grade, the lead horses stumbled off the road. Charley bit down on his cigar and used all his strength to stop the run-away coach, but the terrain was too rough. The wooden wheels nearly splintered when the stage struck the rocky embankment. A wrenching jolt threw Charley from the rig, but he hung on tight to the reins. The horses dragged Charley along on his stomach, but he soon managed to steer the frightened horses back onto the road. Charley had saved all his passengers and was now a bonafide hero.

During the peak of the Gold Rush, many bands of surly highwaymen stalked the roads. These outlaws would level their shotguns at the drivers and shout, "Throw down the gold box!" Charley Parkhurst had no patience for the crooks despite their demands and threatening gestures. The most notorious road agent was nicknamed "Sugarfoot." When he and his gang accosted Charley's stage, it was the last robbery the thief ever attempted. Charley cracked his whip defiantly and the horses bolted. Charley then grabbed his six-shooter, and with bullets blazing, raced away without loss or injury. "Sugarfoot" was later found dead with a bullet wound in his stomach.

Years slipped by and Charley eventually left the risky stage-coach business and took up farming in the Sacramento Valley. At age 64, Charley suffered from painful rheumatism, and later developed cancer of the tongue and throat from years of smoking and chewing cheap tobacco.

On January 2, 1880, the Sacramento *Daily Bee* published Charley's obituary. It read; "On Sunday last, there died near here, a person known as Charley Parkhurst, aged 67, who was well-known to old residents as a stage driver. He was in early days accounted one of the most expert manipulators of the reins who ever sat on the box of a coach. The immediate cause of his death was a cancer of the tongue. It was discovered when friendly hands were preparing him for his final rest, that Charley Parkhurst was unmistakably a well-developed woman. The shocking news could scarcely be believed by persons who had known Charley for a quarter of a century."

Once it was discovered that Charley was a woman, there were plenty of people to say they thought he wasn't like other men. Even though he wore leather gloves summer and winter, many noticed that his hands were small and smooth. Charley slept in the stables with his beloved horses and was never known to have had a girlfriend.

Charley never volunteered clues to her past. Loose fitting clothing hid her femininity and after a horse kicked her, an eye patch over one eye helped conceal her face. She weighed 175 pounds, could handle herself in a fist fight and drank whiskey like one of the boys. J. Ross Browne, Western author and traveler of the period, reported that Parkhurst never drove the day after payday. He was always too tired from drinking all night and gambling for two-bit cigars.

In 1880, the Gold Hill *Evening News* stated, "It is beyond question that one of the soberest, pleasantest, most expert drivers in this city, and one of the most celebrated of the world-famed California stage drivers was a woman." Turns out that Charley's real name was Charlotte Parkhurst. As a child, she was raised in a Massachusetts orphanage, unloved and surrounded by poverty. Charlotte escaped when she was fifteen years old and soon discovered that life in the working world was easier for men. So she decided to masquerade as one for the rest of her life.

The rest is history. Well, almost. There is one last thing. On November 3, 1868, Charlotte Parkhurst, cast her vote in the National Election. She became the first woman to vote in the United States, 52 years before the passing of the 19th amendment!

CHARLEY DARKEY PARKHURST
1812 — 1879

NOTED WHIP OF THE GOLD RUSH DAYS
DROVE STAGE OVER Mt. MADONNA IN
EARLY DAYS OF VALLEY. LAST RUN
SAN JAUN TO SANTA CRUZ. DEATH IN
CABIN NEAR THE 7 MILE HOUSE,
REVEALED "ONE EYED CHARLIE",
A WOMAN, THE FIRST WOMAN TO VOTE
IN THE U. S. NOV. 3, 1868

ERECTED 1955

PAJARO VALLEY HISTORICAL ASS'N.

CHAPTER SIX SELECTED SOURCES

Anne Seagraves, *Women of the Sierra*, WESANNE Enterprises, Lakeport, California, 1990.

George Lyman, *The Saga of the Comstock Lode*, Charles Scribner's Sons, New York, 1934.

Leon Rowland, *Santa Cruz: The Early Years*, 1980.

Lucius Beebe & Charles Clegg, *U.S. West: The Saga of Wells Fargo*, Bonanza Books, New York, 1949.

Eliot Lord, *Comstock Mining and Miners*, Berkeley; Howell – North, 1959.

Mead B. Kibbey, *The Railroad Photographs of Alfred A. Hart, Artist*, edited by Peter E. Palmquist, 1996.

Lucius Beebe, Holiday Magazine, article, *King of the Stagecoach Drivers*, Vol. XIV, September, 1953.

Sacramento *Daily Bee*, January 2, 1880.

Gold Hill *Evening News*, April 2, 1872, January 3, 1880, January 28, 1880.

Weekly Nevada State Journal, August 17, 1872.

PHOTO CREDITS

Page 53   *Harper's Weekly*, September 14, 1878.

Dare to Shoot the Flume

EVERY YEAR, MOUNTAIN BIKERS flock to Lake Tahoe's East Shore, eager to ride the old Flume Trail. Littered with wooden planks from a 19th century water flume, this narrow pathway hugs the steep west slope of the Carson Range. It challenges the courage and endurance of adventuresome cyclists. The ride also rewards the brave with some of Lake Tahoe's most spectacular views. Although a ride along the Flume Trail can stir the heart, the real excitement associated with flumes ended more than a century ago.

Nevada's popular "V flume," so named because it is shaped like the letter "V", was first built by James W. Haines, in 1869. Haines, who later became a Douglas County State Senator, rigged the first V flume to move timber down out of the Carson Range. This inexpensive alternative to the traditional method of constructing roads for horse-drawn wagons, revolutionized the transportation of lumber in western Nevada.

Over the years, many other lumber companies constructed their own flumes to transport water and lumber. Historic records indicate Haines later sued in United States District Court to determine his right to benefit as inventor of the V flume, having patented it on September 20, 1870. However, so many others testified that they had built a flume themselves, Haines lost the case.

The long, winding flumes were built in sections. Each section consisted of two boards 16-feet-long, each two feet wide and one and a half inches thick. The planks were joined together at a ninety degree angle. They were built tight enough to hold water and strong enough to carry heavy logs up to forty feet long. High elaborate trestles supported the flume down inaccessible canyons and across steep-sided chasms, moving the timber quickly and cheaply down the mountainside.

The flume's V-shape had an important purpose. It is designed so that if the sliding lumber lodges onto something, the flowing water will back up, raise the wood along the slanting sides, and free it. The same efficacy is not accomplished in the more traditional U-shaped flume, with its box-like perpendicular sides. In some of the steeper and more arid areas, loggers used dry chutes to move the timber. These were made of cut-out logs, firmly staked together and greased daily. The dry chutes were shorter than the water flumes, but the big logs flashed down so quickly that the friction often produced a bright trail of sparks, fire and smoke.

Once the flumes were built, the sawmills were relocated higher into the mountains, closer to the timber. The flume operation became the most efficient and important transport system utilized to move the wood down to the Virginia City Comstock mines. With the discovery of the Crown Point Bonanza in 1871, followed by other large silver strikes, the demand for lumber increased dramatically.

Unlike the shallow placer gold deposits in the California foothills, the silver in Nevada was found in deep-running veins of decomposed quartz. Some of the silver veins were sixty-feet wide. No miner or engineer had ever seen a lode so pure, or so thick, and that created a problem. No one knew how to mine the silver safely. The rich ore bodies were so soft that no explosives were needed, only a miner's pick. But when the miners tried to dig into the sandy matrix, the walls and ceiling came crashing down on them.

The work was too dangerous and the mines fell silent. Comstock mining engineers could only scratch their heads and ponder the problem. Finally, Philip Deidesheimer, an engineer from Germany, came up with a solution. He invented a wooden support system that used square sets of lumber to create protective cubes. The men could mine the ledges safely within these timbered structures. As the ore was excavated, more square sets were added, until the interior of Mount Davidson resembled the steel-beamed interior skeleton of a modern day skyscraper.

Deidesheimer's ingenious design spelled success for the Silver Kings, but it meant annihilation for the Sierra's majestic pine forest. As additional ore bodies were discovered, more wood was needed to supply the ever expanding mining operations. Then, on October 26, 1875, most of Virginia City, as well as the hoisting works of the principal mines, burned to the ground. The residents and business owners re-built their boomtown with larger buildings, which consumed even more wood. In order to satisfy the high demand for timber, lumber companies hired hundreds of French Canadian, Italian and Chinese laborers to chop wood from April to November. Three new lumber mills were built at Glenbrook, on Lake Tahoe, and experienced mill crews were imported from Maine to operate them.

The V flume proved so effective at delivering the lumber, that by 1879, there were ten of them operating in the Sierra. The longest Sierra flume snaked its way through the mountains for nearly 25 miles. They totaled more than eighty miles in length. In that year alone, loggers flumed more than 33 million feet of lumber. Lumberjacks also floated small wooden boxes, called Go Devils in the flumes. These V-shaped boxes carried tools, supplies and sometimes lunch, from worker to worker.

One of the most spectacular flumes was owned by the Pacific Wood, Lumber and Flume Company. Built on an elaborate wooden trestle, the flume had its upper terminus high in the mountains, north of Lake Tahoe. This engineering masterpiece wound its way for fifteen miles before ending at Huffaker's Station, near the Virginia & Truckee railroad tracks. Located ten miles south of Reno, Granville Huffaker employed 500 men in 1876. The train completed the work by hauling the valuable timber up to the Comstock mines.

An engineering marvel in its day, this massive flume was owned jointly by Comstock moguls — James Fair, James Flood, John Mackay and William O'Brien. Called the Bonanza V flume, it took two million feet of timber and 56,000 pounds of nails to build. Designed and constructed by engineer, John Hereford and his crews, the mammoth project required only ten weeks to build. Construction costs were $250,000. It effectively transported 500,000 feet of lumber per day, which is about 500 cords of wood. It took the sweat and muscle of 2,000 horses to do the same job.

Twentieth century mountain bikers may enjoy the exhilarating descent down from the old Flume Trail, but they really don't know what a wild ride is.

In 1875, an East Coast newspaperman was treated to the trip of a lifetime. H.J. Ramsdell, a New York *Tribune* reporter, was assigned to Virginia City to report on the Comstock. He got more of a story than he bargained for.

While touring the various mining works, Ramsdell asked how the timber was transported out of the mountains. Mining magnate John Mackay suggested a visit to the Bonanza V flume. Two days later, Ramsdell met with James Fair and James Flood in Virginia City. Joining them on the trip was John Hereford, the contractor who built the big flume. The four

men left in two buggies, crossed Washoe Valley, and headed for the timber country north of Tahoe.

Once there, Ramsdell climbed to the top of the trestle-work to see the huge logs roar down the flume. "It was like the rushing of a herd of buffalo." he wrote. "I preferred to view the flume, in active working, from a distance."

After he returned to the main group, Mr. Flood and Mr. Fair challenged Ramsdell to join them in a trip down the flume by hog trough. Hog troughs were crude boats, V-shaped like the flume and sixteen feet long. The 200-pound city reporter could not believe what he was hearing, but he thought that, "…if men worth 25 or 30 million dollars apiece could afford to risk their lives, I could afford to risk mine which is not worth half as much."

The men were well-dressed, but not concerned about their clothes or their lives. It was determined that Ramsdell would join Fair in the first boat with Flood and Hereford in the second. For a bit of comfort, two small boards were installed as seats. At the last minute, Fair decided the party should take along someone who knew something about the flume. There were fifty millhands and lumberjacks standing around, so Fair asked for volunteers. Only one man responded to the call, a red-faced carpenter who took more kindly to drinking whiskey than to working at his bench.

While three stout workmen held the boat over the rushing current, Ramsdell, Fair and the carpenter were told to jump in as soon as the boat was dropped. They were also told to hang on to their hats. One experienced flume shooter warned, "A flume has no element of safety. You cannot stop, you cannot lessen your speed; you have only to sit still, shut your eyes, say your prayers, take all the water that comes…and wait for eternity."

The boat was lowered and at the critical moment the carpenter jumped into the front of the boat, Ramsdell into the stern and Fair into the middle. Suddenly they were off. When the terrified reporter finally opened his eyes, they were already streaking down the mountainside. The trestle was 70 feet high in some places; and, since Ramsdell was lying down, he could see only the aerial flume stretching for miles ahead. Ramsdell tried to judge their speed by watching the hills. "Every object I placed my eye on was gone before I could clearly see what it was," he recalled, "Mountains passed like visions and shadows," and it seemed that they would suffocate from the force of the wind. Suddenly, the first boat hit an obstruction and the drunk carpenter was sent sprawling into the flume, ten feet ahead.

Within seconds Fair dragged the workman back into the boat, but he smashed his hand in the process. "Minutes seemed hours," Ramsdell said later, "I was scared almost out of reason."

Meanwhile, the pig-trough carrying Flood and Hereford was making better time. This second boat crashed into the first and Flood was thrown into the rushing water. The rest of the men hung on for dear life. This confusion of splintered boats and bodies slid the rest of the way to the bottom of the flume. The frightened men fell fifteen miles in just thirty-five minutes, but saved themselves a whole day of traveling by horse-drawn carriage!

When the flume finally leveled out and the men could exit the chute, they were more dead than alive. The carpenter quickly headed to the nearest saloon for a shot of tarantula juice. James Flood declared that he would not shoot a flume again for all the silver in the Consolidated-Virginia mine. James

Fair proclaimed that, "I will never again place myself on an equality with timber."

Reporter Ramsdell was able to write a good story, but his main satisfaction came from the fact that his hosts were so battered and sore, they could not get out of bed the next day.

CHAPTER SEVEN SELECTED SOURCES

William Johnson, *Genoa Flumes*, article in *The Genoa-Carson Valley Book*, by Anthony Amaral, Bicentennial Issue, 1975–76.

W.F. Edwards, *Tourist Guide and Directory of the Truckee Basin*, Truckee, 1883.

Myron Angel, *History of Nevada*, Oakland, California, 1881.

Eliot Lord, *Comstock Mining and Miners*, Berkeley: Howell-North, 1959.

L.J. Ettinger, *The Best of Virginia City and the Comstock*, published by L.J. Ettinger, Reno, 1995.

Nevada State Journal, November 12, 1950, article by Peggy Trego.

Nevada Appeal, March 30, 1975.

Truckee Republican, January 3, 1874.

Hank Monk – King of Stage Drivers

BEFORE RAILROADS put the western stagecoach companies out of business, travel via horse-drawn carriage was the rule. For three decades after 1850, miners, bankers and tourists relied on the rough and ready stage drivers to get them through the mountains safely. Stages ran at all hours, every day. Drivers were usually more concerned with speed than safety, however; and the crack of the whip was heard more often than the squeal of the brakes.

Stage drivers possessed colorful characteristics and ranked as aristocracy on the Nevada frontier. Most wore handsome gloves of the softest leather, finely-stitched gray frock coats and fancy jewelry. Some drivers never spoke; others talked a little just to be sociable, while a few repeatedly told jokes just to see some Easterner bite. All had pride in their occupation and treated their horses like family.

Among the crack whips was Billy Blackmore, known for his devotion to duty and concern for his passenger's comfort. Billy concentrated so much while driving that his evening dreams were often a repetition of his last run. His nightmares always included the steep and dangerous down grades. During his nocturnal rides, he would press down on the foot board of the bed, muttering, "Whoa, there! Whoa!," all the while believing he was bearing down on the brakes. Billy was a terror to landlords, who were forced to build special beds that he could not kick down.

Driver Baldy Green was noted for his bad luck at the hands of highway robbers. His stage was held up so often that Wells Fargo concluded he was either in with the gangs or just plain cursed. Old Baldy was transferred to the Austin drive far out in the Nevada desert. It broke his heart to leave his old route, so he quit driving and moved to Pioche, where he hauled freight for a living.

But Baldy Green's memory lives on in a popular song about this star-crossed Wells Fargo stager.

The Ballad of Baldy Green

I'll tell you all a story,
And I'll tell it in a song,
And I hope that it will please you,
For it won't detain you long;
'Tis about one of the old boys
So gallus and so fine,
Who used to carry mails
On the Pioneer Line.
He was the greatest favor-ite
That ever yet was seen,
He was known about Virginny
By the name of Baldy Green.
Oh, he swung a whip so gracefully,
For he was bound to shine—
For he was a high-toned driver
On the Pioneer Line.
Now, as he was driving out one night,
As lively as a coon,
He saw three men jump in the road
By the pale light of the moon;
Two sprang for the leaders,
While one his shotgun cocks,

$2500
REWARD

On Sunday night, 27th inst., the Stage from Colfax to Grass Valley was stopped by four highwaymen and our treasure box robbed of following amounts:

$7,000 IN COIN.

In a leather pouch, and three packages of coin containing respectively $50, $18 and $10.   We will pay the above

REWARD OF $2500

in Gold Coin for the capture of the robbers and the recovery of the Coin; *or*

$1250 FOR THE CAPTURE
of the Robbers, and
$1250 FOR THE RECOVERY
Of the Coin.
L. F. ROWELL,
Ass't. Supt. of Wells, Fargo & Co.

Saying, "Baldy, we hate to trouble you,
But just pass us out the box."
When Baldy heard them say these words
He opened wide his eyes;
He didn't know what in the world to do,
For it took him by surprise.
Then he reached into the boot,
Saying, "Take it, sirs, with pleasure,"
So out into the middle of the road
Went Wells & Fargo's treasure.
Now, when they got the treasure-box
They seemed quite satisfied,
For the man who held the leaders
Then politely stepped aside,
Saying, "Baldy, we've got what we want,
So drive along your team,"
And he made the quickest time
To Silver City ever seen.
Don't say greenbacks to Baldy now,
It makes him feel so sore;
He'd traveled the road many a time,
But was never stopped before.
Oh the chances they were three to one
And shotguns were the game,
And if you'd a-been in Baldy's place
You'd a-shelled her out the same.

The early mining booms brought so many coach companies to Nevada that it became a cutthroat business. Economics ruled and money went to the coaches that made the fastest time, no matter how reckless the ride. Despite the danger of capsizing, rival stages bounced down the narrow mountain roads, flirting with the steep cliffs. Drivers took curves at breakneck speed, except when the roads were glazed with ice. When trails were slick, drivers tied the rear wheels with rope, which acted as a brake on the perilous down grades. Hardier passengers did not mind the turbulent ride, in fact, they often made huge bets to see which driver could make the best time.

The stages were well-built to handle the rough terrain. The wheels and axles usually held together despite slamming into blocks of stone or lurching in and out of deep chuckholes. The carriage remained intact in spite of the passengers inside, who bounced around like so much ballast, and often wound up in a pile on the floor. The ride for those clinging to the roof was most exciting of all, and most dangerous.

Stage accidents were common, although usually not fatal. Occasionally, tragic accidents did occur. On July 22, 1863, a stage with fifteen passengers on board, nine inside and six outside, toppled over a cliff and rolled into the Truckee River. A few managed to jump to safety, but most were injured and one man was killed. Passenger A. C. Wightman, was thrown into the river and caught by the violent current. The rushing water tore off all his clothes, but rescuers managed to pull him to safety one hundred yards downstream. Another driver and all six horses were killed when a stage flipped over and rolled 300 feet down a steep mountainside. Miraculously, all the passengers survived.

Most famous of all the men who ever handled the reins of a coach was Hank Monk. He was a hard-drinking and a hard-driving man. Tough, courageous and sharp-tongued, he captured the hearts of the people with his heroic feats. So many stories have been told about this popular whip that it is hard to tell fact from fiction. But, when it comes to Hank Monk, the truth alone offers plenty of excitement. This story pays tribute to one of the most enduring legends of the early West.

Henry James Monk was born in Waddington, New York, on March 24, 1826. When he was 26 years old, he moved to San Francisco. Hank had always loved horses, so shortly after his arrival in California, he landed a job driving the stage between Sacramento and Auburn for the California Stage Company. At that time, the California Stage Company controlled ninety percent of the coaching business in California and the Oregon Country, operating 2,690 miles of stage routes in all.

With the discovery of silver and the expansion of mining into the Washoe District of Nevada, the upstart Pioneer Stage Company began running daily coaches from Placerville, California, to Virginia City, Nevada, over a hastily cut road south of Lake Tahoe. Monk later joined the Pioneer Stage Company and took over the Placerville to Genoa, Nevada route. This dangerous route climbed up and over the mighty Sierra and was one of the toughest rides in all the west. Drivers on this rugged trans-Sierra crossing encountered washed-out bridges, ferocious blizzards, lashing rain and stage robbers.

Monk handled the ribbons with consummate skill. People said that he never seemed to be in much of a hurry, but no one who took his stage ever complained about being late. Hank enjoyed the enviable reputation of never having dumped his stage. Most dignitaries and visitors traveling to Carson City and the Comstock were genuinely curious to meet him. For years, Hank drove visitors up to Lake Tahoe during the summer. Hotel proprietors on the beautiful alpine lake paid Hank to tell tall tales for the benefit of the tourists. The stories were good, but most passengers were more interested in hearing about Hank himself.

Hank Monk was well-paid and always meticulously dressed. He wore a wide-brimmed felt hat, canary-yellow driving gloves, a gray frock coat and carried a silver-handled whip.

His fancy clothes were the finest money could buy. Locally, Monk was more celebrated for his drinking ability than his superior driving skills. The phrase "to drink like Hank Monk" still survives in Virginia City saloons. His drinking habits stood out in an era when men consumed alcohol before breakfast and then drank regularly for the rest of the day. Remembered as a man who could drive when he couldn't walk, he was sometimes carried from the saloon to the waiting coach to resume his run.

Philosophically, Hank believed in two things; always be on time and always maintain the proper rate of speed, no matter who the passengers were. For Monk, it did not matter whether his customers were millionaire Silver Barons, world-famous royalty or well-dressed tourists, they were all treated the same. One night, in the early 1860s, Monk was behind schedule. Trying to make up the lost time, he cracked his whip freely over the horses. Despite the murky darkness and rough, twisting road, Hank kept the stagecoach flying. One of the passengers, a corrupt and egotistical judge, commanded Hank to slow down. "I'll have you discharged before the week is out. Do you know who I am, sir?" yelled the judge. "Oh yes!" shouted Monk, "perfectly well. From no fault of mine I'm late, but I'm going to take this coach into Carson City on time if it kills every damned one-horse judge in the Territory."

Over time, Hank Monk's name became a household word in the west. There were songs composed about him, even the famous playwright Joaquin Miller celebrated him in a poem and a play. Late in the summer of 1880, news came that the President of the United States, Rutherford B. Hayes, wanted to visit the Comstock on his way to California. It was a monumental occasion. The Hayes trip was not only the longest journey yet taken by a President in office, it was also the first visit to that part of the country by a Chief Executive.

Hayes and his Presidential party, which included General William T. Sherman, arrived in Carson City on September 7. The next day, the high-ranking dignitaries boarded several carriages for a drive to Spooner Summit, which overlooks Lake Tahoe. The first coach carried President Hayes, General Sherman, Secretary of War Alexander Ramsey and Nevada governor, John H. Kinkead. Sitting in the driver's seat holding the reins, was Hank Monk, who had sobered up for the occasion. For once, Hank took it easy.

Monk drove Nevada stages for more than twenty years. His record of transporting gold bullion without a loss was unsurpassed, as were the speed records he set racing between popular destinations. During one winter snowstorm, drifts covered the road and Monk's stage was running late. In order to keep to his scheduled time, he drove for forty-eight consecutive hours.

Hank Monk's colorful life was local legend in the early west, but one incident launched him into the national spotlight. Monk was a boyish-looking 33 years old on July 30, 1859, and considered a well-seasoned driver on the Genoa-Placerville run. His only passenger that day was Horace Greeley, famous editor, social reformer, supporter of the transcontinental railroad and future presidential candidate. Miners in Nevada revered him.

The road west from Genoa followed up the headwaters of the Carson River, over Luther Pass to Lake Valley, up Myers Grade to Johnson Pass, and down the American River Canyon to Placerville. Monk's stage was making good time on the steep road, but Horace Greeley had a few words for Hank. "Driver," he asked, "can you get me into Placerville this evening by 5 o'clock, because the committee expects me, and I do not wish to disappoint them; this is the last telegraph station and IF YOU ARE NOT SURE, I will send them a message."

Hank knew a challenge when he heard one and he immediately cracked the whip. "I'll get you there," was all Mr. Greeley heard from the driver's seat. The road to Yarnold's Toll House (Kyburz) was a steep down-grade filled with boulders. They made the first twelve miles in fifty-three minutes. Greeley choked on the dust and tried to hold on. At Yarnold's, Monk quickly changed the team of horses and off they charged. They hurtled around blind corners and along narrow mountain trails. The terror-stricken celebrity tapped Monk on the back. "Driver," he shouted into the wind, "I am not particular for an hour or two!" Greeley was a famous and imposing man but Monk was unimpressed. He yelled, "Horace, keep your seat! I told you I would get you there by 5 o'clock, and by God I'll do it, if the axles hold!"

Fortunately, the axles held and Greeley was able to give his anti-slavery speech to a large and enthusiastic audience. Afterward, Greeley was a good sport about the rough ride and he bought Hank a brand new suit of clothes. Over the years, the story was told and revised, told again and embellished, until finally, on March 29, 1866, an unflattering version was read before a laughing Congress in an attempt to discredit Horace Greeley. In 1872, Greeley ran for president of the United States. He lost.

In 1938, the fraternal order, E. Clampus Vitus, dedicated a Placerville memorial to the famous ride. The inscription reads, "To Remember Hank Monk The World's Greatest Reinsman Who Drove Horace Greeley From Carson City To Here In 1859, Making The 109 Miles In 10 Hours." Hank always said he would have made better time if the horses had been faster.

Hank Monk retired on his Wells Fargo pension and enjoyed his waning years as a local legend. He died of pneumonia in Carson City on February 28, 1883. A large crowd attended his funeral where Monk's coffin was decorated with hundreds of flowers. The Reverend G. Davis closed the service with an eloquent truth; "The man who knows his own natural capacities and strives to occupy the position in life best suited to his gifts, however humble, is a man of brains and honest purpose. Too much credit cannot be given a man who follows a humble calling and takes an honest pride in doing all his work well." Hank would drink to that.

CHAPTER EIGHT SELECTED SOURCES

Lucius Beebe & Charles Clegg, *U.S. West: The Saga of Wells Fargo*, Bonanza Books, New York, 1949.

Lucius Beebe & Charles Clegg, *San Francisco's Golden Era*, Howell-North; Berkeley, 1960.

George D. Lyman, *The Saga of the Comstock Lode*, Charles Scribner's Sons, New York, 1934.

Nevada Highways and Parks, article *Riding with Nevada's Famous Stagecoach Driver...Hank Monk*, edited by Donald L. Bowers, Vol. XVI, No. 2, 1956.

Nevada Highways and Parks, article *Hank Monk...And His Adventures with Horace Greeley*, by Effie Mona Mack, Carson City, September, 1947.

Richard G. Lillard and Mary V. Hook, *Hank and Horace; An Enduring Episode In Western History*, Wilmac Press, Georgetown, 1973.

Myron Angel, *History of Nevada*, Arno Press, New York, 1973 reprint.

Ray Allen Billington, *The Far Western Frontier 1830 – 1860*, University of New Mexico Press, Albuquerque, New Mexico, 1956.

The Genoa-Carson Valley Book, article, *Hank Monk Driver*, by Nancy Miluck, Bicentennial Issue, 1975-76.

Holiday Magazine, article, *King of the Stagecoach Drivers*, by Lucius Beebe, Vol. XIV, September, 1953.

Gold Hill *Evening News*, March 28, 1876 & March 10, 1880.

Reno *Evening Gazette*, August 6, 1891.

Daily Nevada State Journal, March 2, 1883.

Carson City *Morning Appeal*, March 4, 1880 & March 3, 1883.

Marysville *Daily Appeal*, July 25, 1863.

San Francisco *Golden Era*, April 15, 1860.

Sacramento *Daily Union*, August 1, 1859.

The Great Verdi Train Robbery

IN ITS HEYDAY, the riches of the Virginia City Comstock Lode supported thousands of miners, shopkeepers and sundry other respectable business people. It also attracted brazen criminals looking for an easy mark.

With so much wealth in clear sight, the risk of robbery was high and the methods implemented as varied as the crimes. Highway road agents would hide out of sight and then ambush miners traveling over the lonely Sierra trails. Gangs of bold, masked men stormed rural banks for their fat payroll deposits. Still other bands targeted the stagecoaches for the Wells Fargo gold box, as well as the watches, money and jewelry of the passengers. Even walking home from the saloon at night could chance a dangerous encounter with one of these unsavory thugs.

By 1869, corporate mine investors and wealthy bankers in San Francisco felt better about the security of their gold and payroll shipments, to and from Nevada. The most valuable cargo was no longer shipped over the Sierra Nevada by horse-drawn stage. It went by iron horse over iron rails. The Central Pacific Railroad Co. now boasted a small fleet of trains running between San Francisco and Reno. To further protect the cash and bullion shipments, Wells Fargo invested in armored express cars. These fortified cars were manned by trained armed guards.

The timing of the railroad shipments was kept top secret, but everyone knew that with so much money at stake, it was only a matter of time before one of the more resourceful gangs staged a train holdup. Due to an increase in robberies, the Wells Fargo stages were now being guarded by two shotgun messengers mounted atop the coach. The messengers were also accompanied by two heavily-armed outriders who followed at a distance. Road agents were increasingly frustrated by all the extra protection.

The daring deed finally occurred on the night of November 4, 1870, the first recorded armed robbery of any train in the Far West. Surprisingly, the well-planned crime was masterminded by A.J. "Big Jack" Davis, a respected Virginia City businessman. Sometime during the summer of 1870, "Big Jack" and an experienced band of thieves decided to pull off the first Wells Fargo train robbery. Comstock residents and law enforcement officers had no idea that Jack Davis was the ringleader of an extensive and powerful criminal gang. For years, Davis and his masked accomplices had robbed countless stages near Huffaker's Station, along Six Mile Canyon and on the Geiger Grade. Big Jack even had a crazy plan to empty the vaults at the Bank of California in Virginia City.

For the gang's armed ambush on *Atlantic Express Train No. 1,* Davis chose Verdi, Nevada, a small station east of Truckee, California. Isolated deep in the Truckee River Canyon, Verdi was the perfect spot for a robbery. *Train No. 1* was hauling passengers as well as a Wells Fargo express car loaded with newly-minted $20 gold pieces. The coins were part of the Yellow Jacket Mine payroll, but there were bundles of banknotes and piles of silver dollars as well. The shipment was valued at nearly $50,000.

The nature, value and size of a Wells Fargo shipment was usually a well-kept secret, but "Big Jack" outwitted everyone. He sent an advance man, John Chapman, down to San Francisco in order to keep an eye on the payroll shipments leaving for Nevada. When Chapman heard of this extremely valuable cargo, he sent a coded telegram to his contact, Sol Jones, who was staying at the Capital House in Reno. Jones deciphered the message and then quickly rode off to notify the rest of the gang. "Big Jack" and his men were holed up in a cave on Peavine Mountain, north of Verdi. The cave faced south and from there the men could see the Central Pacific train tracks.

Train No.1 departed Oakland in the early morning darkness of November 4, 1870. In Sacramento, train crews added more engines for the long haul up the Sierra's west slope toward Donner Pass. *Train No. 1* was delayed below Cisco by the twelve-car derailment of a westbound freight. *No. 1* finally rolled into Truckee at 10 p.m., two hours late. Passengers aboard the comfortable Silver Palace Car were told that they might as well get out and enjoy the gambling and saloons in Truckee.

Train No. 1 did not pull out of Truckee until after midnight; but, Marshall, the Wells Fargo messenger, was not too concerned. He knew that it was a fast and easy downgrade all the way to Reno where Nels Hammond, the Reno agent for Wells Fargo, would give him a receipt for the shipment. Marshall could relax after that.

Engineer Henry Small had his fireman toss a few lengths of pine into the firebox and then stoked up the boiler pressure. It wasn't long before the train was roaring down the Truckee River Canyon. Near the Nevada border, Engineer Small slowed the train for its scheduled stop in Verdi. The water tanks would be topped off and more wood loaded into the tender car for the long journey across Nevada. With a loud hiss and a belch of black smoke, the lurching train screeched to a stop at the lonely station.

The night was cold and a light snow was beginning to fall. Suddenly, two masked men in long linen dusters appeared out of the darkness and confronted Conductor Frank Mitchell on the train platform. The men were hiding shotguns under their dusters, so they were able to coax Mitchell back inside at gunpoint. "Big Jack" and the other men who had been hiding in the shadows jumped onto the train. Armed to the teeth with six-shooters and shotguns, the bandits easily overwhelmed the frightened train crew.

"Big Jack" ordered the hostages onto the floor of the Palace Car. He then told Engineer Small to take the train about a mile down the track and stop again, but before Small could comply, one of the bandits crouched down on the rear of the express car, cut the bell cord and pulled out the coupling pin. The boiler was fired up and *Train No. 1* roared ahead, pulling only the tender and the gold-laden express car. The baggage and Silver Palace Car were left behind, stranded on the tracks.

The brakeman was the first to realize that the engine and express car had been hijacked. He ran to the call box to request help by telegraph, but again "Big Jack" proved to be a worthy adversary. The telegraph wires had been cut fore and aft of the stranded train. The lines were dead. Davis knew that it would take someone an hour or more to find a working call box. He planned to use that time wisely.

Davis forced the engineer to drive the train several miles to a stone quarry where the balance of his gang waited. Upon their arrival there, Small was shoved towards the locked door of the Wells Fargo Express car. Marshall was still inside, well-armed and ready to shoot it out for the gold and silver. Engineer Small, however, was in no such position. He was staring down the muzzles of loaded guns and under threat of death. The terrified engineer managed to convince Marshall to open

the door without a fight. Reluctantly, Marshall surrendered. "Big Jack" thanked him kindly for not giving them any trouble. Otherwise, they would have had to kill him.

The bandits used axes to break open the Wells Fargo strong boxes heaped full of gold coins. They counted out $41,600, which was quickly divided. They dumped the gold coins into special purses they had made from boot-tops and buckskin. "Big Jack" took $20,000 for his efforts, secretly buried the booty, and then rode south for Virginia City. Several of the gangsters took the road north to Crystal Peak, where they buried the heavy and troublesome gold in a ravine. The rest scattered in different directions.

The robbery itself was quite successful; the result of careful planning and quick execution by a team of eight daring men. But their perfect crime was soon spoiled by an inquisitive woman. That night, gang member, John Squires, took lodging at the Sardine Valley House, just north of Verdi. This tavern and small hotel was operated by Nicholas Pearson and his wife, quiet, law-abiding citizens who were not part of the crime ring.

A couple of hours later, two more bandits, E.B. Parsons and James Gilchrist, registered and took a room across the hall from Squires. Minutes later, Squires quietly crossed the hall and entered the other room. Mrs. Pearson noticed the suspicious activity and climbed the stairs. Putting her ear to the closed door, Mrs. Pearson heard the three men whispering and she decided to keep an eye on them.

Early the next morning, Squires and Parsons rode off, leaving Gilchrist behind. By now, Mrs. Pearson had heard of the big train robbery from a customer and sensed the trio's uneasiness. When Gilchrist left his room carrying a heavy sack, Mrs. Pearson played the sleuth in earnest. She quietly followed him to the outhouse, where she peeked at him through a small knot hole. She watched him pour $20 gold pieces into an old boot which he lowered into the latrine. Mrs. Pearson knew then that Gilchrist was one of the bandits. She quickly ran back to the house and sent her husband for the sheriff.

Later, a group of armed hunters arrived. Mrs. Pearson convinced them of Gilchrist's involvement in the holdup and he was quickly surrounded. After Deputy Sheriff James Kinkead rode up and arrested Gilchrist, Mrs. Pearson showed him an unusual bootprint she had seen in the fresh snow. It had a narrow heel, the kind popular with gamblers and dudes. Sheriff Kinkead was impressed; he had seen the same imprint in the snow near the stone quarry.

Just hours after the crime, Central Pacific and Wells Fargo offered a $40,000 reward for the arrest and conviction of the daring robbers. The gang had set a dangerous precedent and both companies wanted to dampen any enthusiasm for a repeat performance. The big reward acted as a powerful magnet for police officers and private detectives from both California and Nevada. Within hours, John Squires was arrested in Sierraville, with his fancy boots held as evidence. It turned out that Squires already had a long history as a stagecoach robber.

After his arrest, Gilchrist spilled the beans and implicated "Big Jack" Davis. Another gang member, Chat Roberts, also turned State's evidence; and within four days the eight men involved in the scheme were in custody. All the loot save $3,000 was recovered. The gang enjoyed a short trial at the Washoe City County Court.

On Christmas Eve, four members of the gang were sentenced from 18 to 22 years in the State Prison. A twenty-year sentence was leveled on known stage robber John Squires. E.B.

Parson, a long-time Virginia City gambler, also got twenty. Tilton Cockerell, a known gun man and road agent, was sentenced to 22 years hard labor. John Chapman, a Sunday School superintendent, was sent away for 18 years. The judge reduced Sol Jones' sentence to five years for cooperation and James Gilchrist and Chat Roberts went free for testifying against the others.

Despite his role as gang leader, "Big Jack" Davis was sentenced to only ten years in prison. That lesser sentence was later cut to three years by the governor. He was released in two years due to his reputation as ex-superintendent of the San Francisco Mine, and as a good citizen of the Comstock. Actually, there were several reasons for "Big Jack's" early discharge from prison. Davis had been arrested in Virginia City and then brought down to Washoe City for his hearing. After the hearing, the guards were ordered to take Davis back to the Virginia City jail. As they climbed the steep Ophir Grade, they came up behind a 12-oxen team pulling two heavily-laden wagons. Near the top of the hill, the trailing wagon suddenly broke free. Jack Davis shouted a loud and timely warning for the guards to jump and save themselves. No one was hurt. His warning yell earned him some gratitude from law enforcement and local citizens.

In September, 1871, Cockerell, Chapman, Parson, and Squires led a violent prison break. Although Cockerell was never seen again, the rest were quickly captured. Davis was given a break for his lack of complicity in the breakout, and was pardoned for saving the life of a prison guard in another breakout four years later. But "Big Jack" never learned his lesson. In his first year of freedom, he was killed in White Pine County while attempting to rob a Wells Fargo stage coach. The sensational train robbery finally passed into history when gangster E.B. Parsons was pardoned in November, 1881.

This story of the first western train robbery should end here. Unfortunately for the passengers onboard *Train No. 1*, it did not. Just 20 hours after "Big Jack" and his bandits had scattered into the dark Sierra night, *No. 1* was robbed again. Another gang of men hit the train at the small station of Independence, east of Elko. An unknown number of armed men employed the same strategy as the gang in Verdi. They broke into and then looted the Wells Fargo express car filled with registered letters and packages. Mr. Johnson, the Wells Fargo messenger, heard the bandits coming and managed to hide $10,000 under the train's woodpile. The robbers forced Johnson to open the safe, but there was only $3,100 in it.

Satisfied with their haul, the bandits fled across the desert. When Elko's Sheriff Fitch and his deputies arrived on the scene, they found a glove with the name Edward Carr on it and a brass locket with the name and company of a soldier named Harvey. These men were two of six soldiers recently deserted from nearby Camp Halleck. Wells Fargo offered $5,000 in reward money for their arrest, conviction and return of the loot. Sheriff Fitch and a large posse hunted the bandits for two days, but a lack of clues and an approaching snowstorm forced them to temporarily give up the search. When the pursuit resumed, it included special Central Pacific trains, a troop of United States Calvary from Fort Halleck as well as a number of deputies and detectives.

Three of the railroad robbers were finally apprehended near the Great Salt Lake. None of those caught were the deserters from Fort Halleck. Dan Taylor, Leander Morton and Daniel Baker were all found guilty of robbery on January 13, 1871. Although the indictment by a U.S. Grand Jury insisted they be hanged, all three were sentenced to thirty years imprisonment. Five months later, fugitive gang member, Lee Morgan, was captured by Detective Porter Rockwell. Morgan even had the incriminating evidence on him. He had just pulled $4,000 in gold coin from a cache. Unfortunately for him, he never got the chance to spend it.

As for the eastbound passengers on *Train No. 1*, it may have seemed that the wild west was getting a little too exciting.

CHAPTER NINE SELECTED SOURCES

Mead B. Kibbey, *The Railroad Photographs of Alfred Hart, Artist*, edited by Peter E. Palmquist, 1996.

Nevada — The First Hundred Years, Sponsored by Harold's Club, Great Western Publishing Co., Reno, Nevada, 1964.

Lucius Beebe & Charles Clegg, *Virginia & Truckee: A Story of Virginia City and Comstock Times*, Berkeley; Howell–North, 5th edition, 1963.

Lucius Beebe & Charles Clegg, *U.S. West: The Saga of Wells Fargo*, Bonanza Books, New York, 1949.

Virginia City *Territorial Enterprise*, November 6, 1870.

Reno *Crescent*, November 5, 1870, Nov. 12, 1870, Nov. 26, 1870, December 3, 1870 & January 21, 1871.

Nevada State Journal, November 23, 1870, December 17, 1870, Dec. 24, 1870, January 28, 1871, May 27, 1871, July 15, 1871, November 5, 1950 (article by Peggy Trego) & December 11, 1966.

Gold Hill *Evening News*, April 2, 1872.

The Record Run of Bucker Plow No. 9

THE WINTER OF 1890 ranks as one of the worst in Sierra history. Extreme cold combined with unprecedented snowfall to create a season of hardship and heroism.

The Sierra Storm King launched his assault in early November; and by January the situation was desperate. Nearly forty feet of snow had fallen at Emerald Bay before the end of January. That month a derailment in the mountains shut down Central Pacific railroad traffic for fifteen days. It took 4,000 men from Sacramento and Reno two weeks to shovel out the rails. Blizzard conditions inflicted severe frostbite; and avalanches took several lives before the army of snow shovelers were able to break the blockade.

On January 30, the hard work of the engineers and railroad crews finally paid off. When the rails over Donner Summit were nearly cleared, railroad officials focused on the snowbound tracks between Truckee and Reno. This spectacular train route runs through the rugged Truckee River Canyon. Steep embankments and hair-pin turns abound in the tortuous ravine. Deep drifts covered the tracks to depths of ten feet, but Central Pacific was determined to open the line immediately.

The railroad men of the Truckee Division were also anxious to get this last section of track cleared. These heroes of the iron rails were true frontiersmen and extraordinary feats that would break ordinary men were their daily bread and butter. It came as no surprise that there were plenty of burly volunteers for the dangerous job of clearing the snow-packed line from Truckee to Reno.

Charlie Garcia, chief engineer of the Truckee Division, was chosen to supervise the run. Everyone watched intently as he carefully hitched up the powerful locomotives behind a massive 19-ton plow. This plow, known as *Bucker #9*, was so big it took eight engines to ram it through the drifts. Garcia and his fireman then climbed into the first engine behind old *#9* and stoked-up the boiler pressure. Huge volumes of smoke and steam belched forth from the engine and billowed into a dark narrow cloud behind. From their perch high in the cab, the men could see the miles of shifting snowdrifts that loomed before them.

Railroad men called a job like this a "suicide run" because ramming a snowbank was like hitting a stone wall; they were never sure they would survive the impact. The sweating, smoking locomotives were backed up half a mile to gain running room. On signal, all throttles were thrown open and the train roared down the track. Garcia and his men braced firmly for impact as *Bucker #9* barreled into the first snowdrift at forty miles-per-hour.

The plow's iron sheathed wedge penetrated the frozen white wall with tremendous force. The sound of wrenching steel was deafening; and ice and snow flew 50 feet in wild disarray. Huge chunks of snow shattered the glass windshield and poured into the lead engine cab. The thick wall of snow stopped the train dead and pinned Garcia and his fireman helplessly to the rear firewall.

Chief Garcia could not reach the reverse lever so he gave a long pull on the brake whistle and waited for the other engineers to cut their power and back up. But Chief Garcia had underestimated the enthusiasm his men had to make this death

defying run. Long-time conductor "Old Blaney" was in command of the second engine. Blaney laughed when he saw his boss frozen to the wall. He shouted, "Garcia has got his cab window smashed and he's squealing for brakes; let's give him hell!" He backed the train up again and then shoved the throttle forward.

"Old Blaney" ordered the train to full speed, which sent them careening recklessly down the steep Truckee River Canyon. The train's shrill whistles pierced the air in dire warning as *Bucker #9* shredded through the snowdrifts.

The train raced past Boca, California, so fast that the people of that town saw only a blue streak in the snow. In the little hamlet of Clinton, Nevada, there was a small store located near the tracks. When the store manager heard the whistles shrieking in the distance, he opened the front doors to protect the glass panes from the thrown snow. The train shot by so fast, however, that the whole building was filled with the white stuff.

With Blaney at the helm, they blasted the 35 miles to Reno in a record time of 67 minutes. The townspeople of Reno ran cheering to the snow-streaked train, ready to welcome the brave railroad men who had broken the blockade. But "Old Blaney" had no time to receive kisses and praise. He was last seen running for his life in the other direction, chased by his frozen boss, Chief Garcia, who was ready to give Blaney his own version of hell.

CHAPTER TEN SELECTED SOURCES

Mark McLaughlin, *The Great Sierra Snow Blockade*, article in *Weatherwise Magazine*, December 1992/January 1993.

Daily Nevada State Journal, January 25, 1890.

The Amazing Nellie Bly   11

ARLY ON THE MORNING of January 21, 1890, a young news
paperwoman for the New York *World* ran down the gang-
plank of the Pacific steamship *Oceanic* and gratefully set foot
onto a solid, California pier. The stormy Pacific Ocean had
made the crossing rough, but the *Oceanic* still made good speed
from Hong Kong. Nellie Bly had nearly accomplished her fantastic journey, but time was quickly running out. Nellie was
racing to beat Jules Vernes' fictional voyage depicted in *Around
the World in Eighty Days.*

In her attempt to circumnavigate the globe, the intrepid
Ms. Bly shipped out eastbound from New York to London
on November 14, 1889. In Amiens, France, Jules Verne met
Bly at the train station. The famed novelist was anxious to
meet the young lady who was bringing his story to life. He
wasn't the only one. In France, the interest in Nellie's journey grew so intense that Verne's book was reissued in no less
than 10 new editions.

Nellie Bly traveled by mail train to Brindisi, Italy. From
there she boarded the British steamer *Victoria* and sailed
through the Mediterranean, the Suez Canal, and eventually
on to India. The attractive young journalist received no less
than two marriage proposals while on board. She spent Christmas Day in Hong Kong, but her mind was on New York.

By the time Nellie reached San Francisco, the bold twenty-
three-year-old journalist had used up 68 days. Speed was of
the essence. Crowds of Californian well-wishers welcomed
her arrival with cheers and boisterous enthusiasm.

Unfortunately for Nellie, the news she received upon landing was not good. She had intended to take a Central Pacific train over Donner Pass, through Truckee, and then via the Union Pacific railroad to Chicago. From Chicago it was a straight run back to New York City. But now, at the last minute, there was an obstacle to her success. It was the Great Sierra Snow Blockade. Blizzards, avalanches and train derailments had shut down all train traffic over the Sierra Nevada for the past seven days. When Nellie asked Central Pacific's management about the blockade, the embarrassed officials could only say they had no idea when the line might re-open. It was the worst storm in Central Pacific's railroad history.

Her second problem was the "Nellie Bly Escort Corps." The corps consisted of her New York editors, John J. Jennings and W.B. Hopsun, as well as other professional associates from the East. The members of this elaborate delegation were trapped on the eastern side of the Sierra. The New York *World's* welcoming committee had crossed the entire continent only to be stranded in Reno. It seemed to Nellie, that after circling most of the globe, a California snowstorm was going to foil her success as a real-life Phileas Fogg.

All was not lost, however. Nellie's editor, Jennings, had been traveling two days in advance of his associates who were still held up in Reno. Jennings' train had gone several miles past Truckee before railroad officials shut down all west-bound traffic. After forty-eight hours trapped in a snowbound passenger train, the frustrated editor decided on a radical course of action.

He convinced Central Pacific officials to let him ride on a rotary snow plow that was about to clear the rails between Blue Canyon and Alta. At first, the rotary rolled along smoothly, throwing snow in a thick plume. But they had not

gone far when a terrific roar sounded from the towering mountains. Almost instantly the entire machine was buried under an avalanche of snow and rock. Every window in the cab was smashed, but luckily no one was hurt. To Jennings' dismay, however, the rotary was declared out of commission.

This latest obstacle did not stop the dogged New Yorker. His determination to bypass the blockade and meet his favorite reporter was astounding. Despite sober advice for Jennings to remain with the disabled rotary, the resourceful city editor pushed on. He bought himself a pair of eight-foot-long wooden skis, the first he had ever seen. He later said that, "It was like learning to skate — one runner would dart off in a southerly direction while the other would head for the north or west. I slid, and stumbled and fell, but after a time I could travel very smoothly."

Jennings hired a guide to lead him through the snow-choked mountains. The two men traveled all night in the bitter cold. Several times they were nearly swept away by avalanches. The next morning, Jennings broke past the blockade and boarded a California-bound train. Still carrying his new skis, Jennings stated, "I have seen snow and blizzards in New York, but the people back there don't know what snow is."

Meanwhile, Nellie had decided that she would not wait for Central Pacific's valiant, but futile efforts to raise the blockade. She boarded a specially chartered Southern Pacific train which headed east toward Sacramento and then south. After some quick telegraph messages between Jennings and Ms. Bly, the two parties met at Lathrop, near Stockton, California. They detoured by the southern rail route via Barstow and Arizona in order to circumvent the stubborn Sierra blockade. For the thousands of Americans reading about the drama in their hometown newspapers, the tension was electric. Fear that the

altered train route would ruin Nellie's tight schedule cropped up in the headlines, but all went well with her remaining connections. In Chicago, Mr. Jennings and Ms. Bly boarded the *Atlantic and Pacific Flyer Express* train. The *Flyer* averaged 60 miles per hour in its race across the country.

Nellie Bly arrived back in New York City on January 25, having traveled 72 days, 6 hours, and 11 minutes in her epic, world-circling journey. It seemed that everyone in the "Big Apple" wanted to congratulate the daring young reporter.

There is one interesting sidebar to this story. On the same day Nellie Bly sailed for Europe, John Walker, proprietor of *Cosmopolitan Magazine*, announced that he was sending Elizabeth Bisland in a westward attempt to outdo Bly. Bisland, a former colleague of Bly's at the *World*, boarded a train for San Francisco shortly after Nellie shipped out. Bisland's attempt to beat Bly went well until she arrived in England. Although Ms. Bisland was only 3,000 miles from New York City, powerful winter storms racing across the North Atlantic Ocean were hampering steamer traffic from London to New York. Heavy snow and hurricane-force winds were coating ships in thick ice and several crewmen had slipped to their deaths. The severe weather trapped Ms. Bisland in London, where time and fame escaped her grasp.

Nellie Bly was more than just a young, flamboyant reporter. She was a professional woman a century ahead of her time. Born Elizabeth Cochran, on May 5, 1864, she began writing for the Pittsburgh *Dispatch* newspaper at age nineteen, for $5 a week. Later she was earning $25,000 a year with her pen.

As an investigative reporter, Nellie went to extraordinary lengths to develop her stories. In order to expose the horrid conditions in mental asylums, she feigned insanity and engineered her own commitment to Bellevue. Among her many exploits was an excursion into the ocean depths via a diving bell and a daring ride in a hot air balloon. She later became the first woman to report from the Eastern Front in World War I.

Her personal life was difficult and after her husband of fifteen years died, she lost much of her money. Despite his death, she maintained her courage and continued to work for the New York *Evening Journal*. In her popular Sunday column, Ms. Bly reported on social problems of the day; among her concerns were the rights of the workingman, the plight of the unemployed and the power of union activism. She also supported women's emancipation and their right to vote, as well as the protection of children.

Nellie Bly died on January 27, 1922. At the time of her death many considered her the best reporter in America. The *Associated Press* stated that her life was "more active than falls to the lot of more than one woman in ten thousand."

The day after her death, a fellow journalist devoted his column to Nellie Bly. He wrote, "...her life was useful and she takes with her from this earth all that she cared for, an honorable name, the respect and affection of her fellow workers, the memory of good fights well fought and of many good deeds never to be forgotten by those that had no friend but Nellie Bly. Happy the man or woman that can leave as good a record."

Nellie always said, "Energy rightly applied and directed can accomplish anything." It could have been her epitaph.

CHAPTER ELEVEN SELECTED SOURCES

Mignon Rittenhouse, *The Amazing Nellie Bly*, Books for Libraries Press, Freeport, N.Y., 1971, c. 1956.

Brooke Kroeger, *Nellie Bly, Daredevil, Reporter, Feminist*, Times Books, Random House, 1994.

David Ludlum, *Early Railroading over the Snowy High Sierra*, article in *Weatherwise Magazine*, December, 1973.

The New York *Times*, November 15, 1889, January 19, 1890, January 23, 1890, January 26, 1890, & January 28, 1922.

The Sacramento Bee, January 21, 1890.

Nevada State Journal, February 1, 1890.

The Swim from Deadman's Point

MOST VISITORS gape in awe at first sight of Lake Tahoe. It takes time for the mind to absorb the sheer size of this magnificent alpine lake. Suspended high in the Sierra Nevada, Lake Tahoe is an aquatic jewel, 22 miles long and 12 miles wide.

In the late 1800s, tourists splashed and played in the Lake's shallow waters, but no one strayed far from shore. It was commonly believed that the clear, cold water would not support a human body. Indeed, locals pointed out how logs quickly sank in the frigid water and that the bodies of drowned victims were rarely recovered. Water temperatures near freezing prevent tissue decomposition and the buildup of organic gases. Bodies in Lake Tahoe do not float back to the surface.

Inevitably, a daredevil disproved the misconception by swimming far out from shore. Doctors in fog-bound San Francisco were soon prescribing summer vacations at sunny Lake Tahoe for their patients suffering from consumption (tuberculosis) and other congestive diseases. The dry mountain air and fresh water were thought to possess curative properties.

There were many theories as to the depth and formation of Lake Tahoe around the turn of the 20th century. Some believed that the lake was bottomless. Others felt that the basin was the remnant of an ancient volcano. It took a 19th century lawyer/journalist, by the name of Charles F. McGlashan, to prove the first of the theories wrong. McGlashan was the owner/editor of the *Truckee Republican* newspaper. In 1880, he published the first history on the Donner Party.

McGlashan spent a lot of time at Lake Tahoe, so one summer he tried to answer the question of its true depth. He took an empty champagne bottle and tied some twine around the neck. After filling the bottle with buckshot, he rowed out to find the bottom of the vast lake. After weeks of soundings and research, he declared that Lake Tahoe was 1,645 feet deep.

Years later, the U.S. Coast Guard and Geodetic Survey utilized state-of-the-art sonar equipment to probe Tahoe's depths. Incredibly, the modern data verified McGlashan's earlier conclusion. Today we also know that Lake Tahoe consists of ancient glacial melt and seasonal precipitation trapped between two mountain ranges. The only outlet is the Truckee River.

Decades passed before someone attempted to swim across Lake Tahoe. The first to try and succeed was Mrs. Myrtle Huddleston, a world class swimmer and mother of a fifteen-year-old boy. She had previously set the women's world endurance record by staying afloat eighty three and a half hours. Now she wanted to conquer Lake Tahoe.

At 8 a.m., August 24, 1931, Mrs. Huddleston slipped into the chilly water near Deadman's Point, Nevada. Her destination was Tahoe City, California, thirteen miles away. Myrtle's skin was coated with a thick layer of specially prepared grease to help ward off the effects of swimming in the sixty-degree water. In order to save her strength, Myrtle swam slowly, using no more than twenty strokes per minute.

The lake was calm for the first few hours, but during the afternoon, the prevailing southwest wind grew blustery. When white caps appeared, the crewmen in the three escort boats positioned their crafts to block the waves. Despite their efforts, Myrtle was blown seven miles off course. Hour after hour she fought the brutally cold waves that threatened to break her will. Late in the afternoon the wind subsided and Tahoe's surface grew calm again. Myrtle Huddleston renewed her attack, but was so tired, she could not go faster than one mile per hour. Sometime around midnight, Myrtle increased her stroke and pulled away from her rowboat escort. Myrtle had no idea that she was swimming alone in water 1,000 feet deep.

For several hours the escort convoy could find no trace of her. Her trainer and manager, S.A. Yoho, was anxiously waiting for Myrtle at the Tahoe Tavern in Tahoe City. When Yoho heard of her disappearance, he jumped into a speed boat to search for the lost swimmer. Mrs. Huddleston was found just before dawn, feeling ill and discouraged. She had been swimming for more than twenty hours.

The high altitude was really taking its toll on Huddleston and the detour had added seven more miles to her swim. She was ready to give up. At this point, her son Everett, rowed to her side and said, "Mother, hold fast. We are only two miles from shore." His encouragement renewed her vigor and soon Myrtle could hear the cheers and laughter emanating from the large crowd on the Tahoe Tavern pier.

At 7 a.m., Mrs. Huddleston emerged from the icy water. Myrtle laughed when she saw a stretcher waiting on the beach for her. "What's the bier for?" she asked calmly as she walked into the hotel to claim her $700 in prize money. After the presentation, Myrtle said, "Catalina was easy compared to this." Four years prior in 1927, Mrs. Huddleston had swum the thirty-six miles across that channel in twenty hours and forty-two minutes, despite a strong tide against her.

Myrtle's twenty-mile swim in Lake Tahoe had taken 22 hours and 53 minutes. She lost twelve pounds in the ordeal, but later said that despite the hardships of cold water, altitude and wind, she felt no ill effects from the swim.

The first man to conquer the width of Lake Tahoe was William Long, a 27-year-old long distance swimmer from Van Nuys, California. Strong southwest winds carried him off course too, but he managed to stroke the 17-mile swim in just 12 hours. The record was set on August 8, 1955, when Fred Rogers, a 29-year-old bartender from San Francisco, swam from Cave Rock, Nevada to Meeks Bay, California, a distance of nine miles, in just six hours and 46 minutes.

Earlier that summer, Rogers had attempted the "impossible" feat of swimming the length of the Lake. That attempt failed and the lake's 22-mile axis remained unconquered. But Rogers felt so good after his swim on August 8, that he decided to try the length one more time.

On the morning of August 28, 1955, Rogers stepped into the water at King's Beach, on Tahoe's north shore. He was joined by 39-year-old Jose Cortinas, a famous Cuban-born long-distance swimmer. Both men were coated with lanolin before they entered the frigid water. Mile after mile the two men were neck and neck, swimming fast, at nearly 70 strokes a minute. Rogers and Cortinas ate candy bars and sugar cubes and drank orange juice to keep up their strength. They kept up the torrid pace for eighteen miles.

Rogers pulled ahead of Cortinas in the last few miles. There were two rowboats and one power pilot boat escorting the two men. When Rogers took the lead, the power boat was forced to abandon Cortinas to keep up with the leader. Controversy followed the race when Ms. Marlan Boone, publisher of *Water Sports Magazine,* claimed that the pilot boat had not only abandoned Cortinas, but had led him off course as well.

Rogers, however, was unaware of the confusion and kept increasing his lead. Near the end of the race Rogers suffered from severe leg cramps and was ready to give up until Mr. Long, president of the Lake Tahoe Swimming Association, swam out to cheer him on. Long shouted, "You've got it made. Don't hurry. The world record is in sight!" Rogers stopped and floated awhile to gain strength, before he pushed on past the finish-line flags at Bijou. He completed the "impossible" swim in 19 hours, six minutes, and six seconds.

There were four hundred fans waiting for Fred on the beach. Smiling, he said, "I suffered leg cramps, but when I found out how close I was; I gave it all I had." Cortinas stroked to shore at Bitler's Point, four miles away. Cortinas was exhausted and rushed by ambulance to Tahoe Village and put under medical attention. Considering the waves and current, it was estimated that Rogers swam more than 29 miles.

Unfortunately, neither man qualified for the $2,000 prize put up by the Lake Tahoe Swimming Association. Even though the men entered the contest under the association's rules, neither had paid the $300 entry fee.

CHAPTER TWELVE SELECTED SOURCES

Joanne Meschery, *Truckee: An Illustrated History of the Town and its Surroundings*, Rocking Stone Press, Truckee, California, 1978.

Edward B. Scott, *The Saga of Lake Tahoe*, 9th edition, Sierra-Tahoe Publishing Co., 1980.

Myron Angel, *History of Nevada*, Oakland, California, 1881.

Truckee *Sierra Sun*, August 11, 1955.

Lake Tahoe News, September 1, 1955.

Daily Nevada State Journal, August 24, 1931.

Nevada State Journal, August 9, 1955, August 30, 1955, September 1, 1955.

Reno Evening Gazette, August 24, 1931.

Gift Books

Personalized, autographed books make great gifts anytime of the year. When ordering your book(s), please include the recipient's name (printed clearly), as well as the preferred mailing address for shipping the book. To order a personally autographed book signed by author Mark McLaughlin, please mail your check or money order with correspondence to:

Mic Mac Publishing
P.O. Box 483
Carnelian Bay, CA 96140

MAIL ORDER PRICES

Western Train Adventures: The Good, the Bad & the Ugly
$18.95 plus $5.00 S & H

Sierra Stories: True Tales of Tahoe — Vol. 1
$9.95 plus $3.95 S & H

Sierra Stories: True Tales of Tahoe — Vol. 2
$9.95 plus $3.95 S & H

*Shipping and handling charges are good for any one to three items.
*Discounts available on volume orders.
*Orders shipped to California must have appropriate sales tax added.

FOR MORE INFORMATION

Be sure to visit our website at <www.MicMacMedia.com> or call 530.546.5612 for the most current list of available books and other products.